Calm Suns

∞ solace ∞ soothe ∞ cheer ∞ comfort ∞

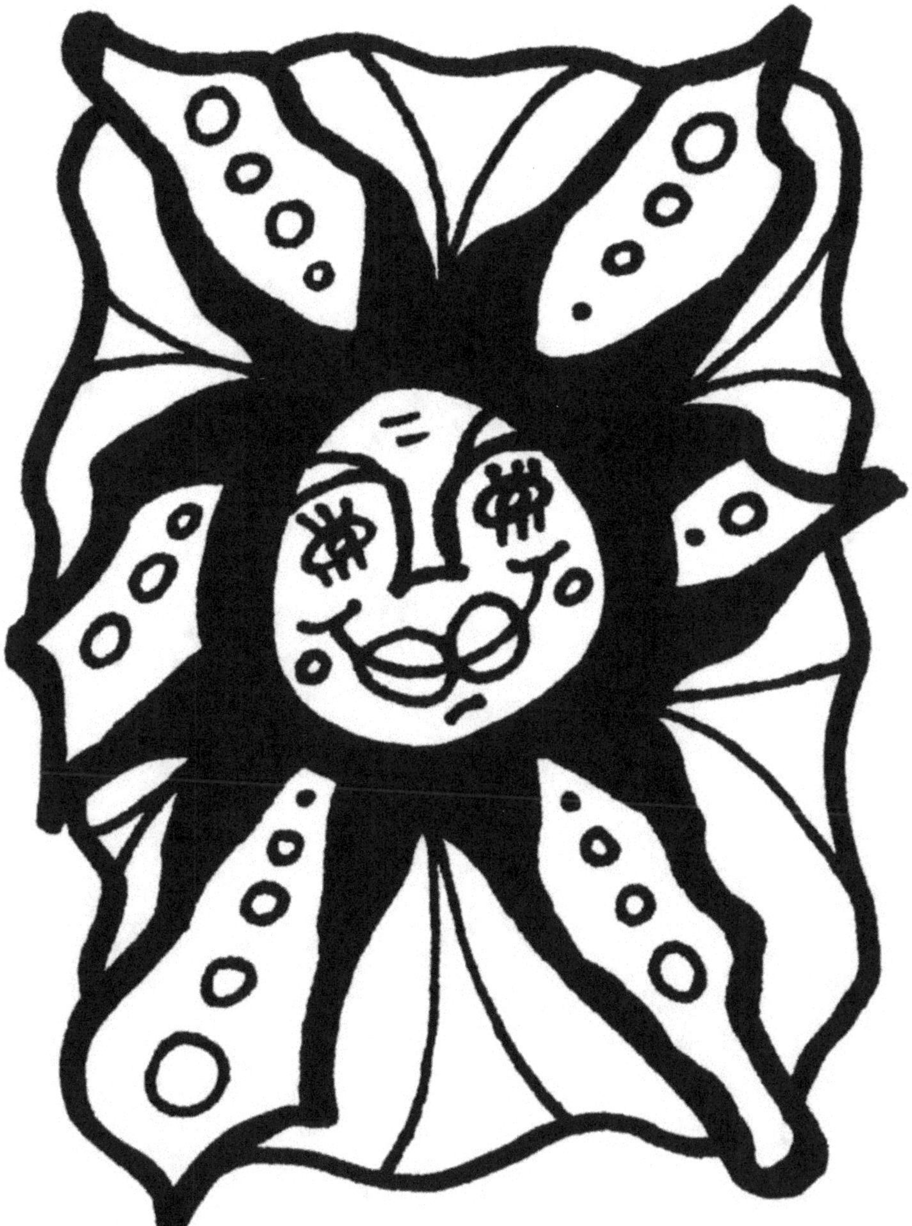

"A Larger Design Coloring Book"

Jenny Carlisle Carrington

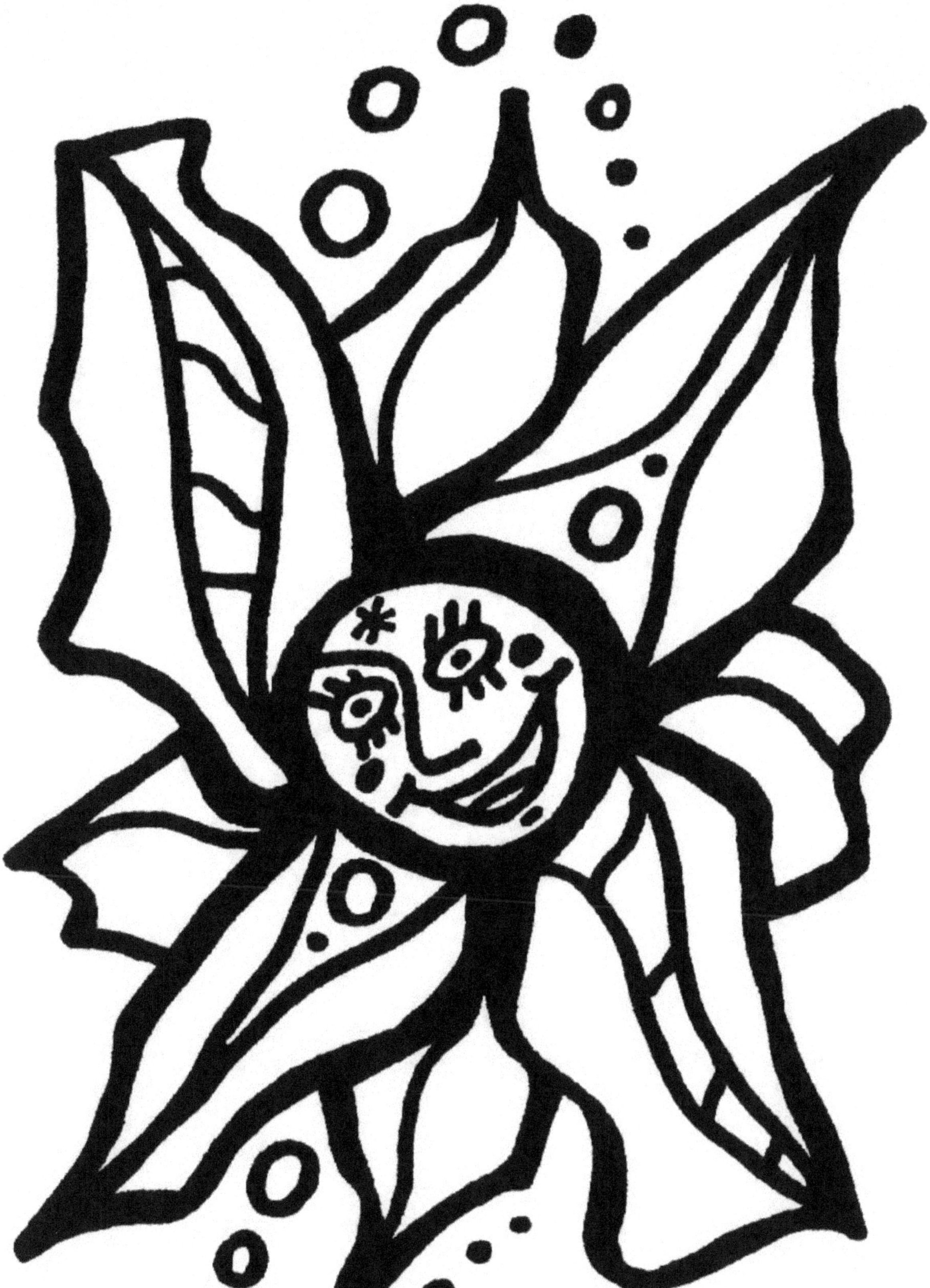

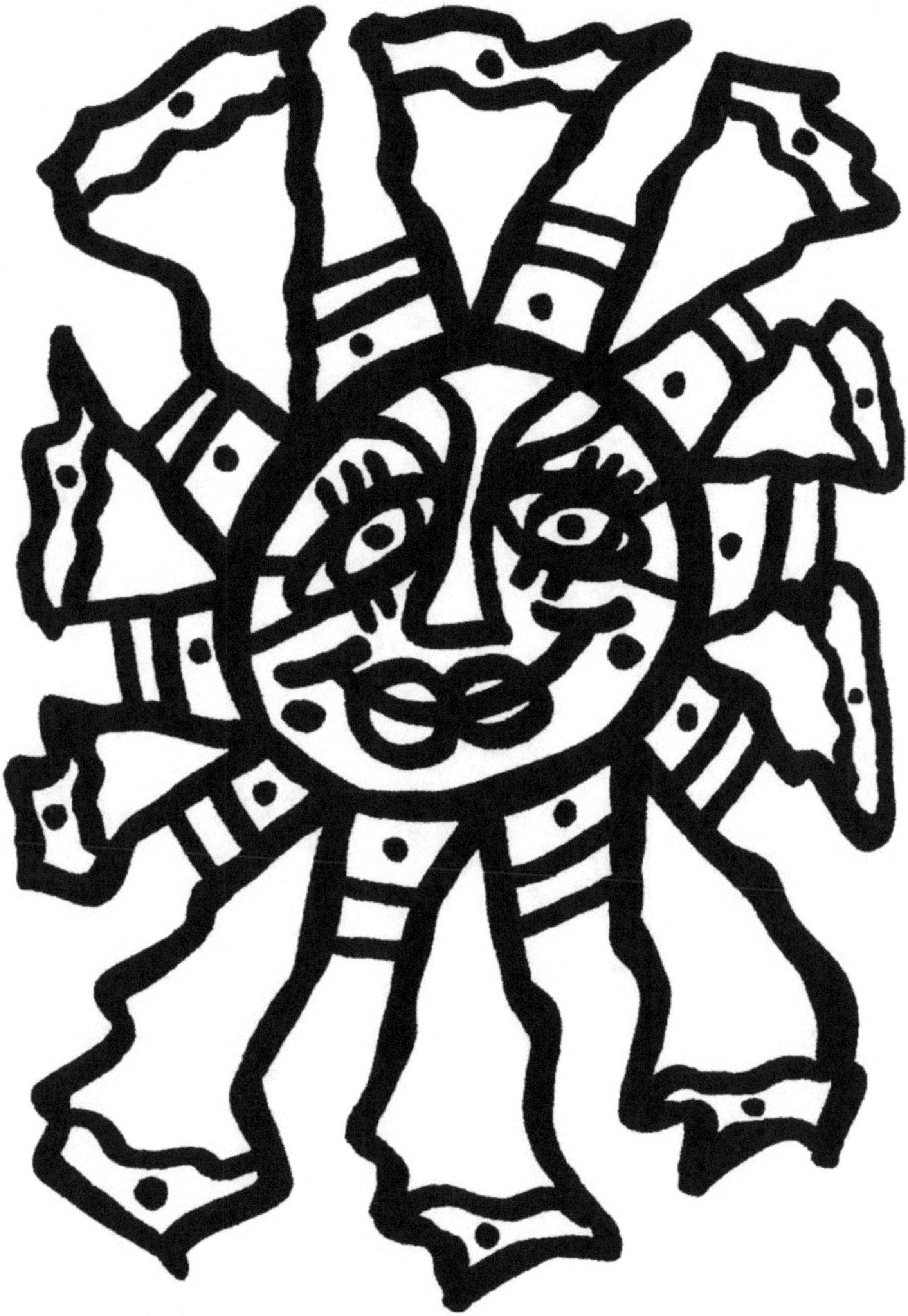

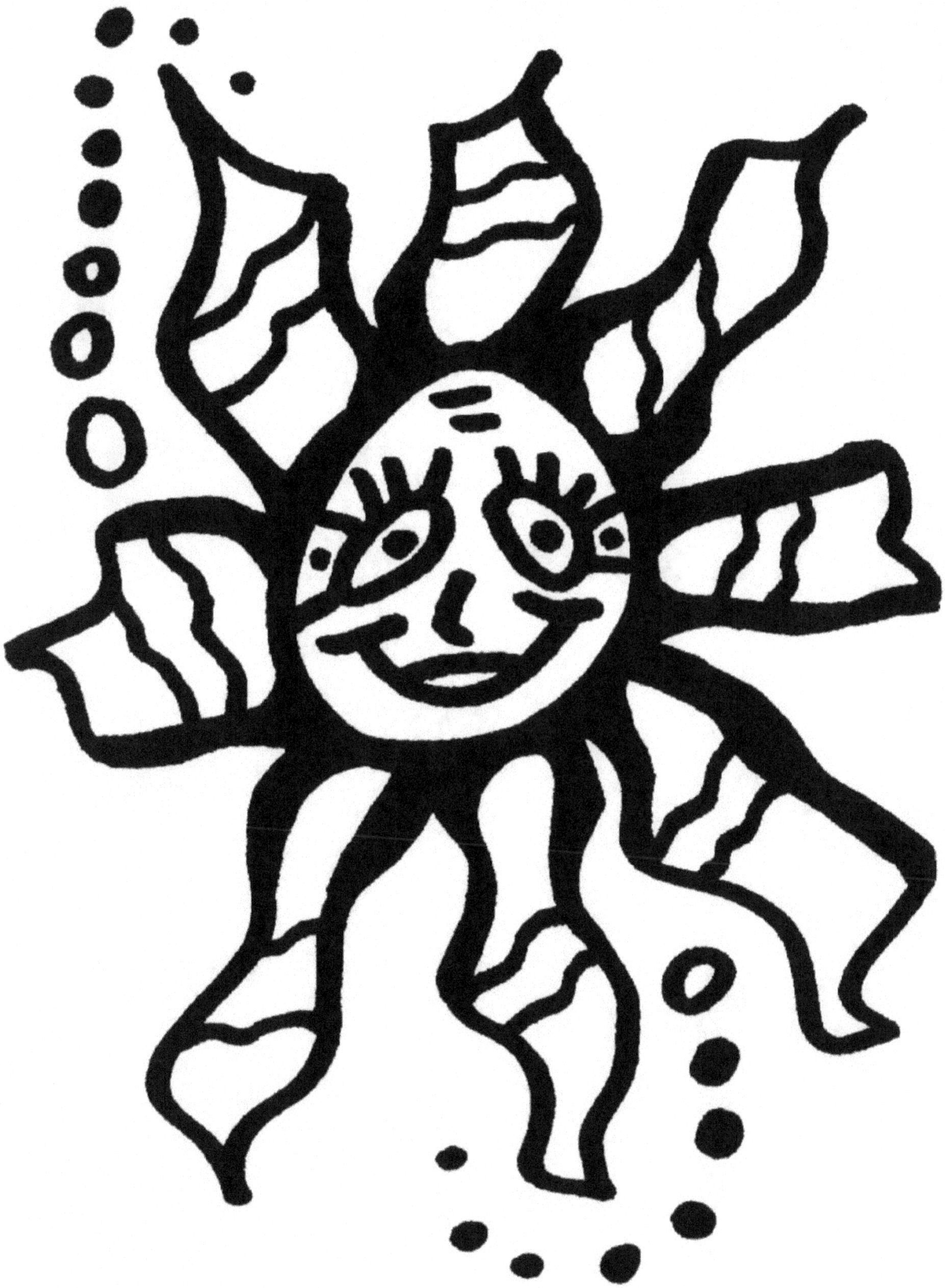

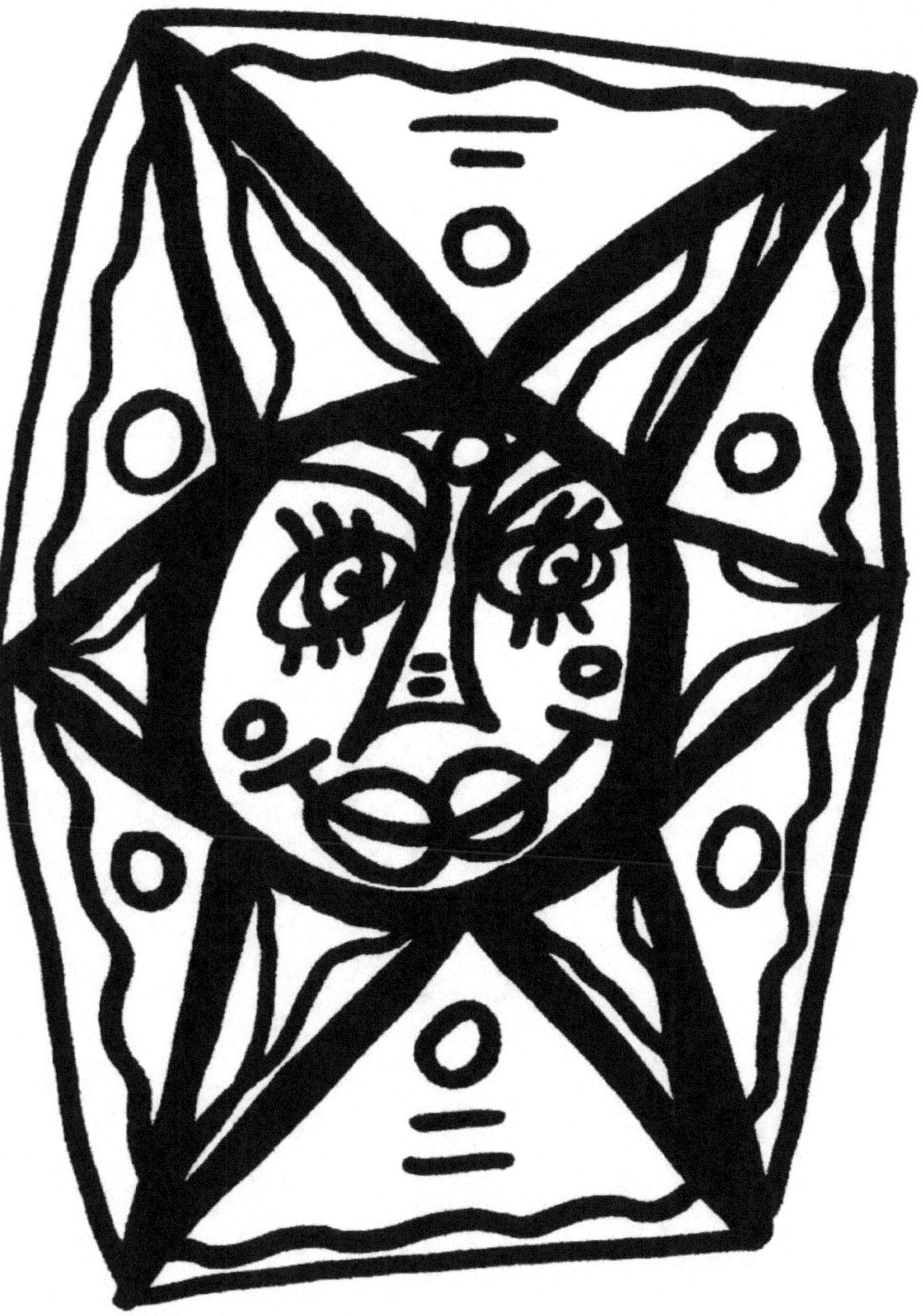

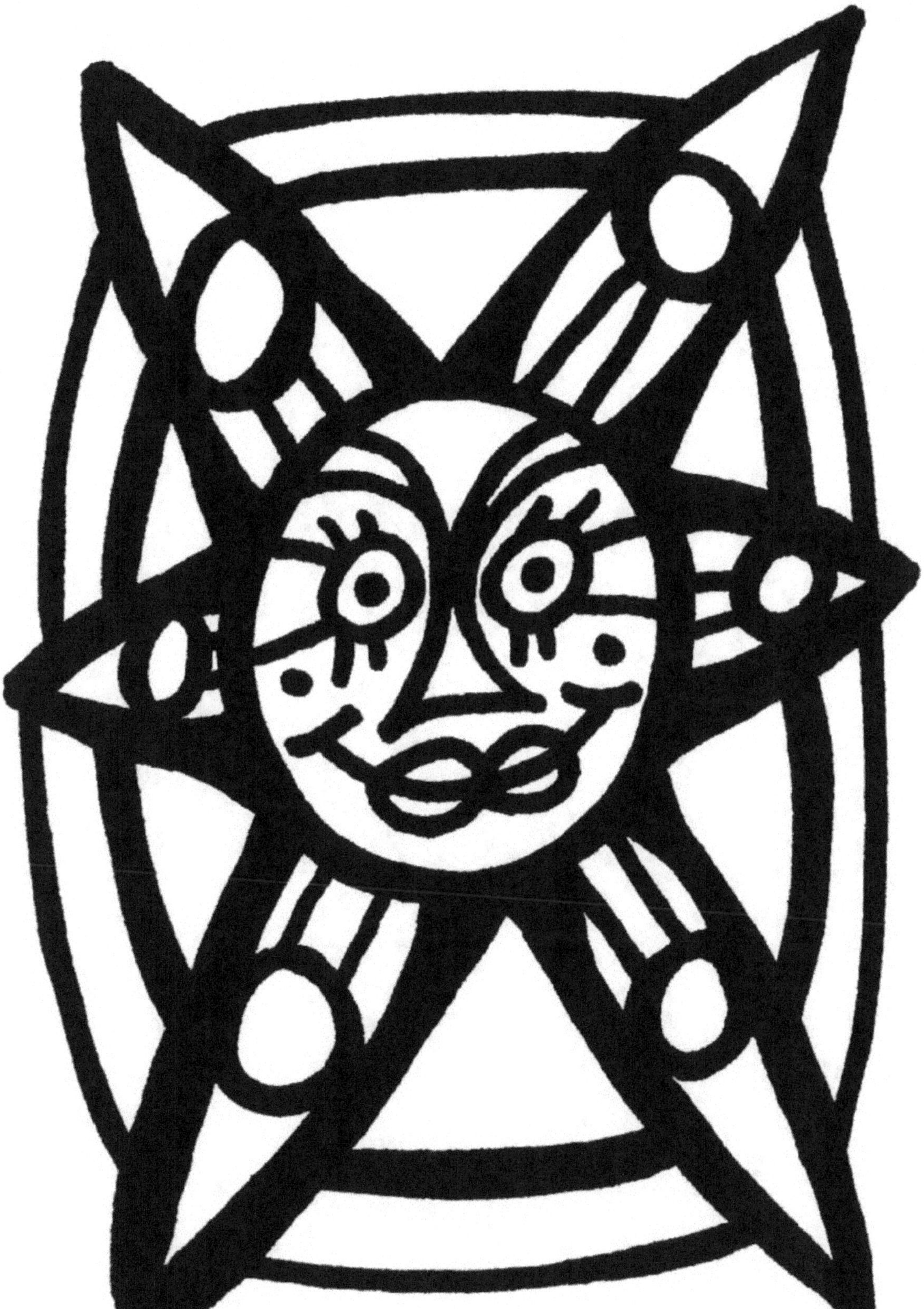

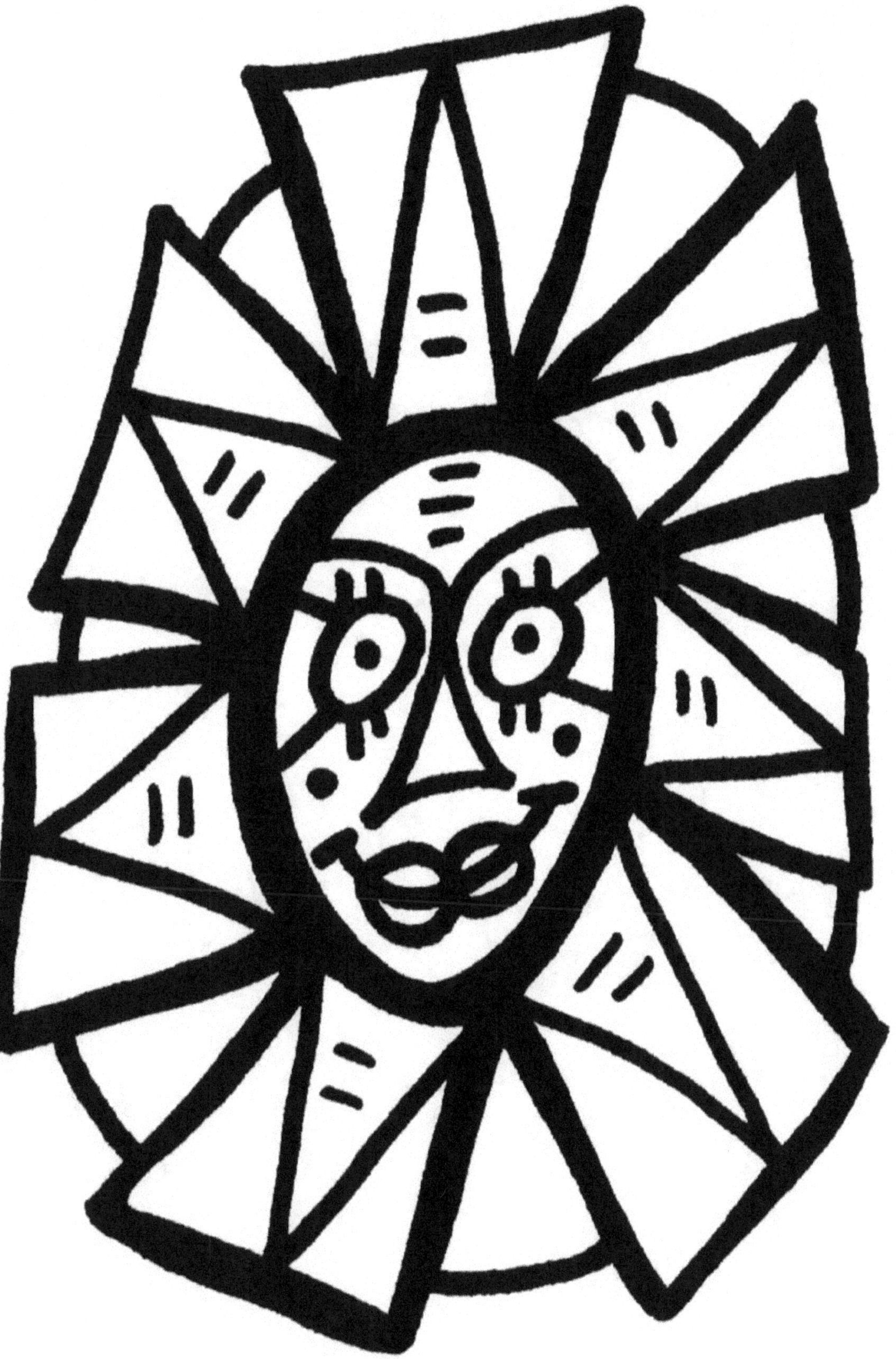

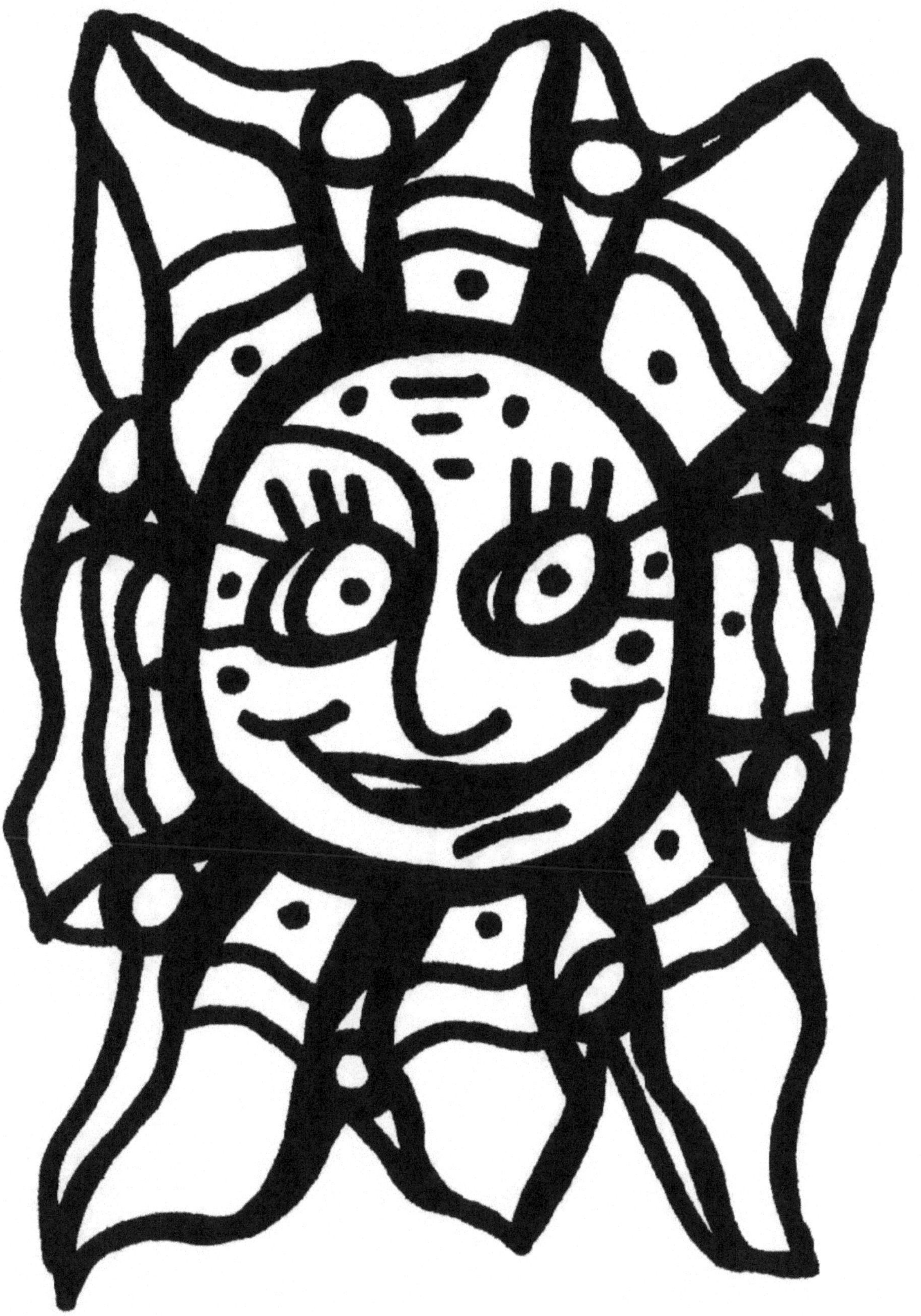

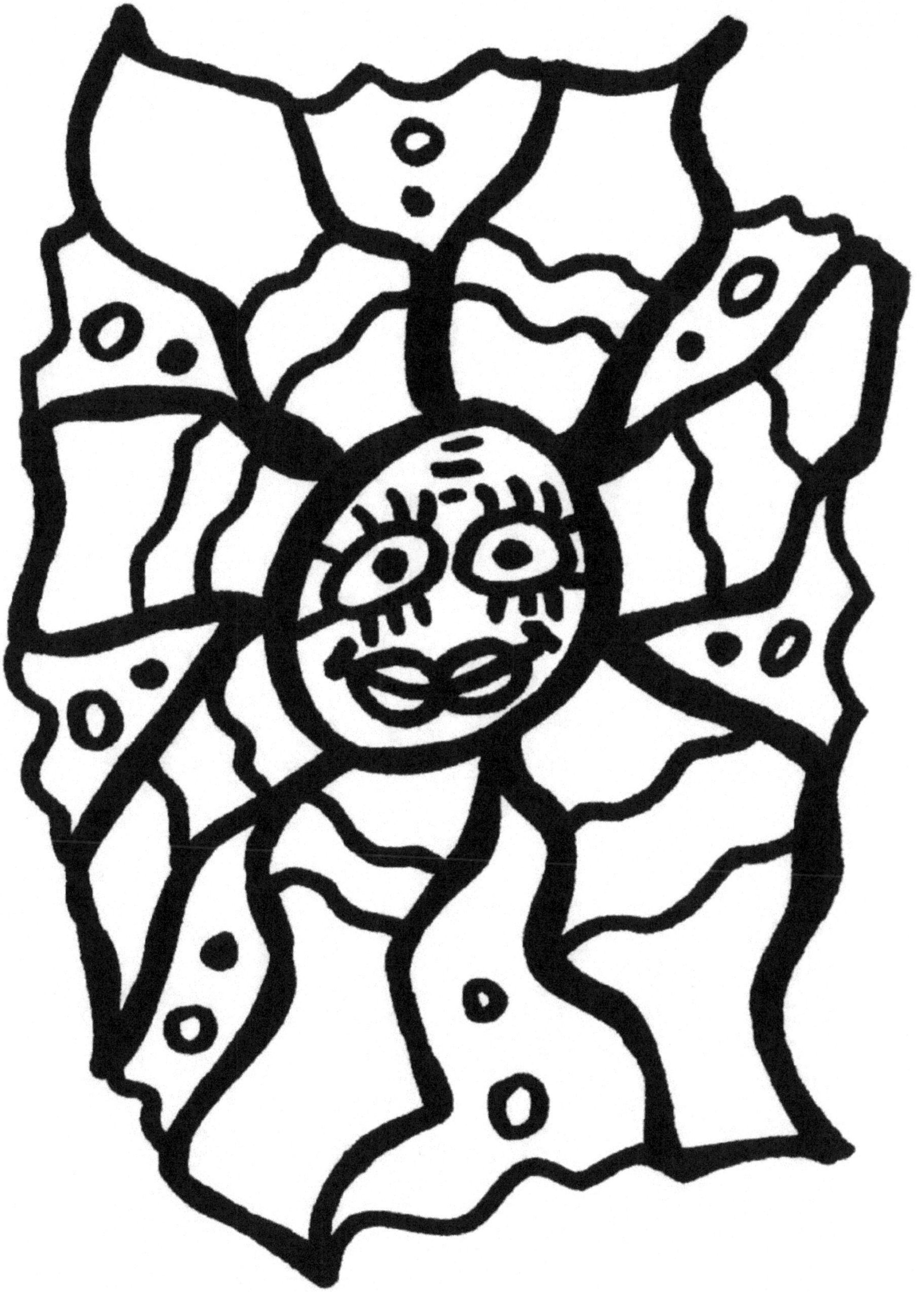

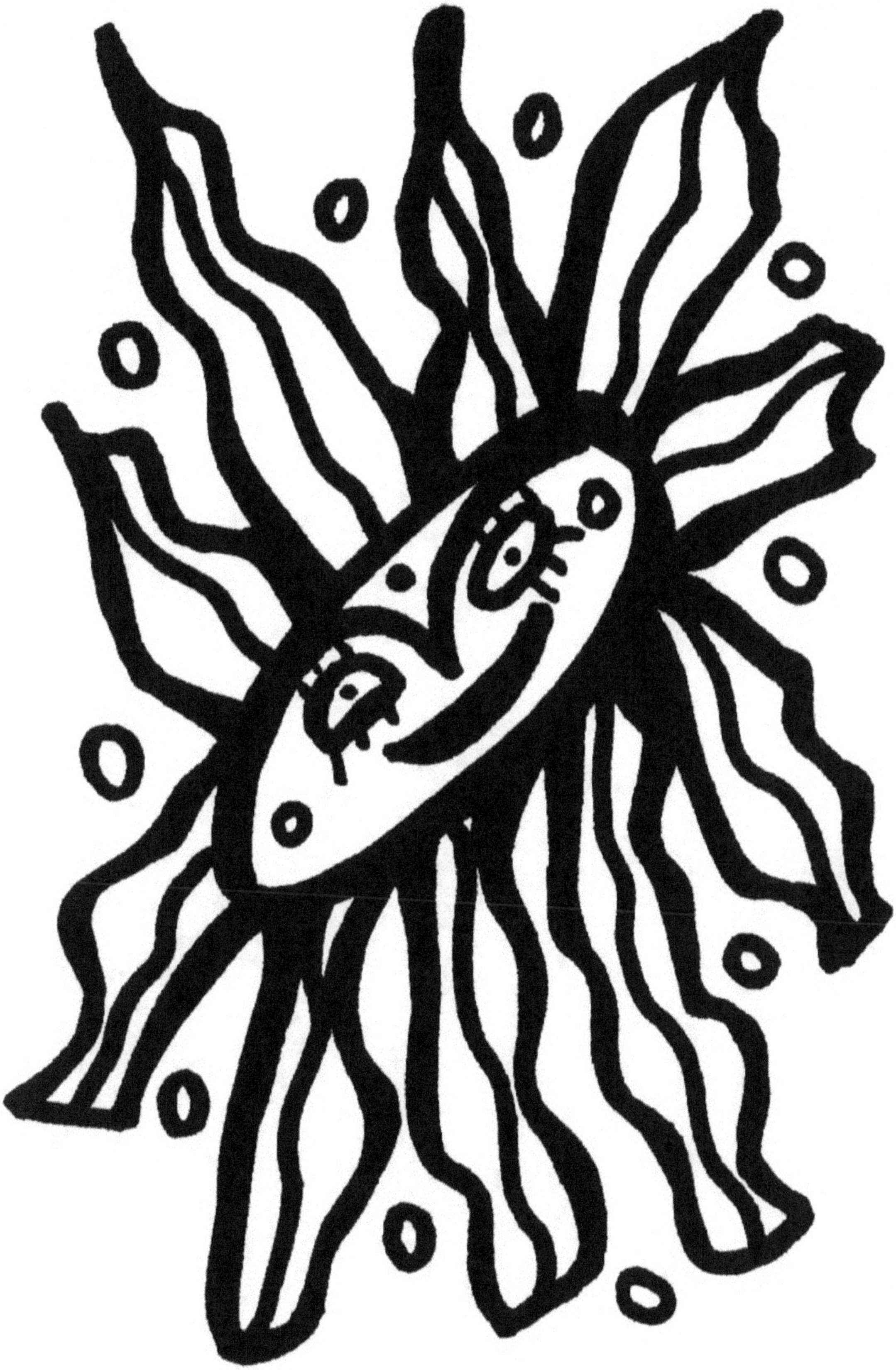

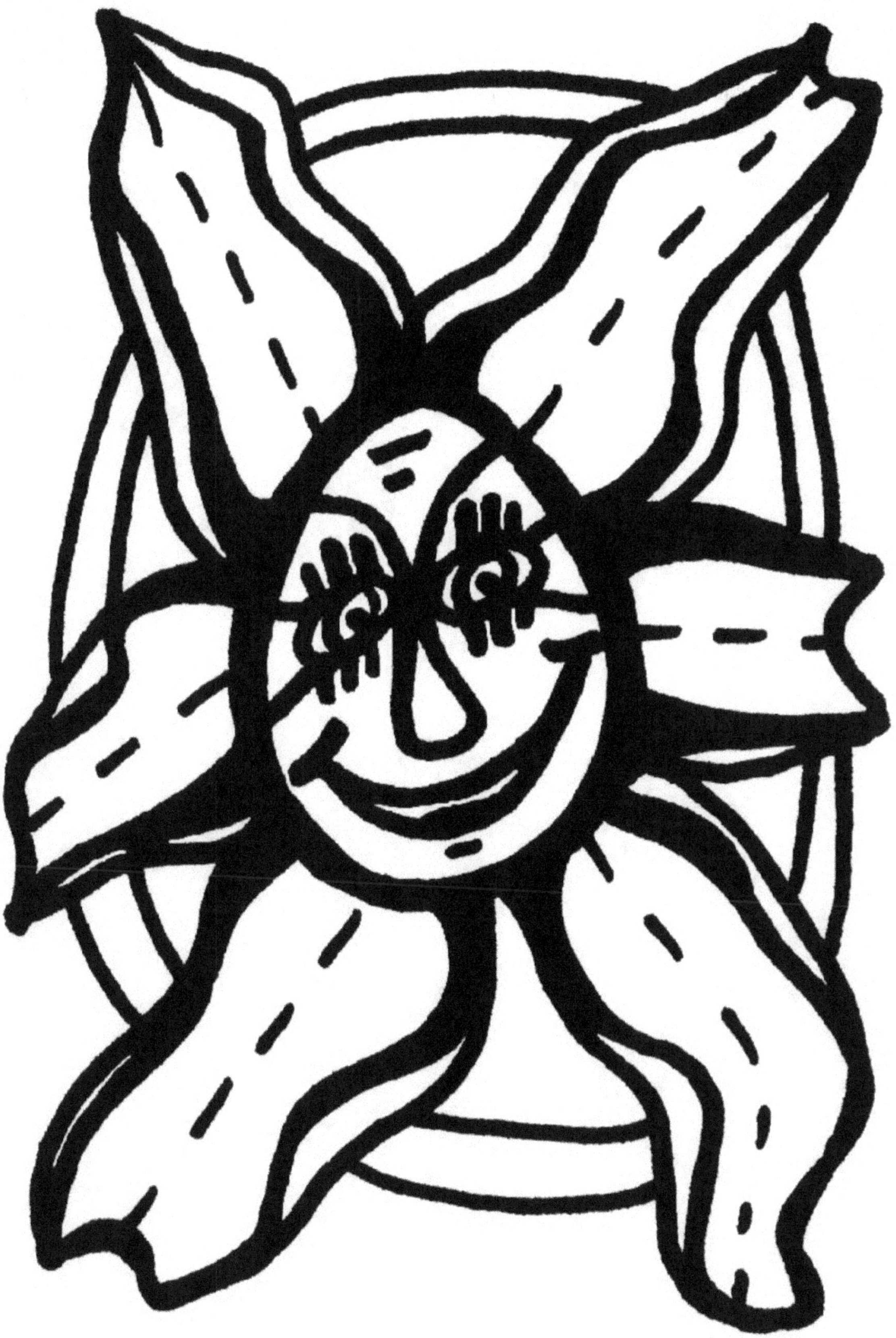

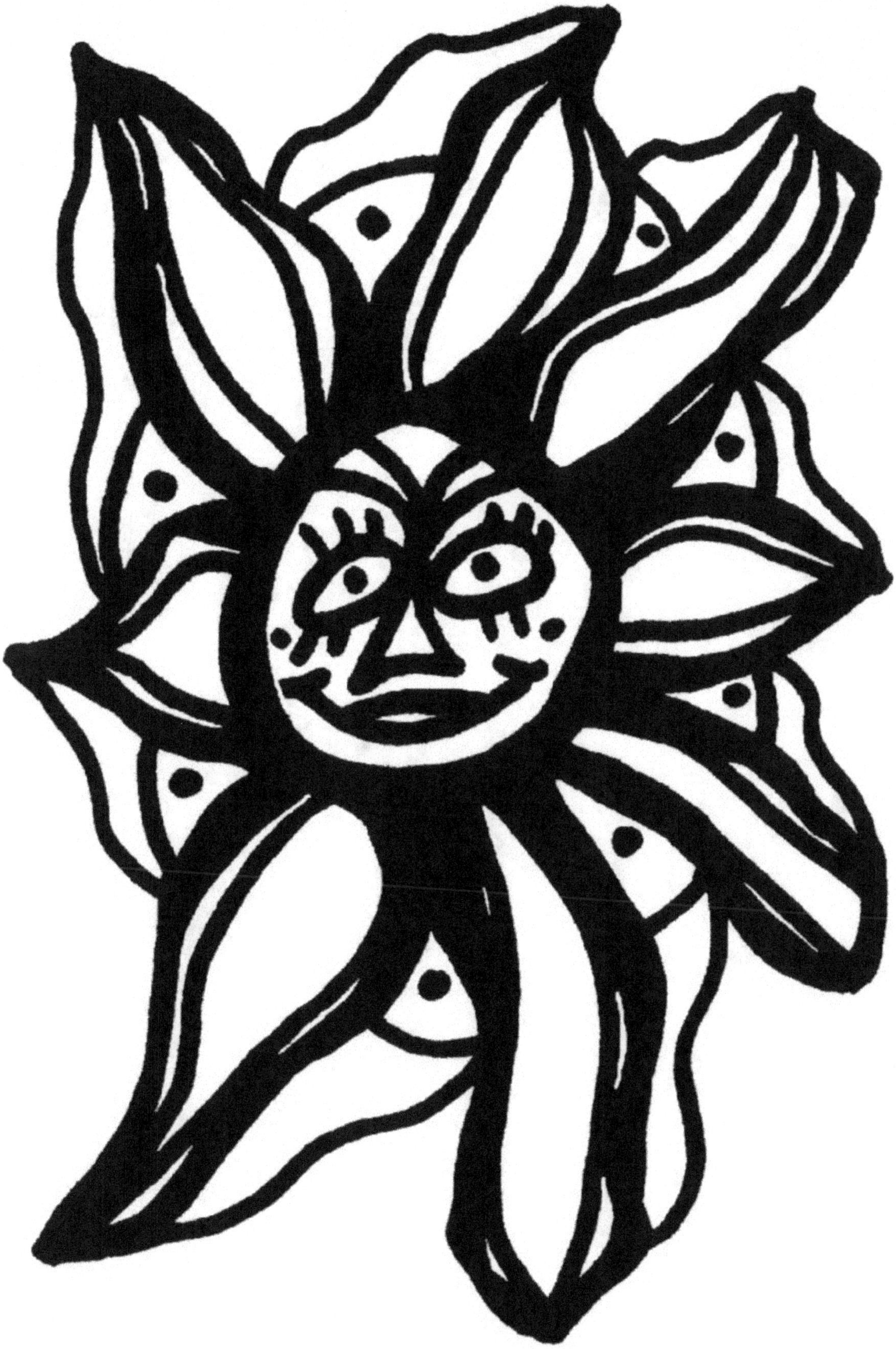

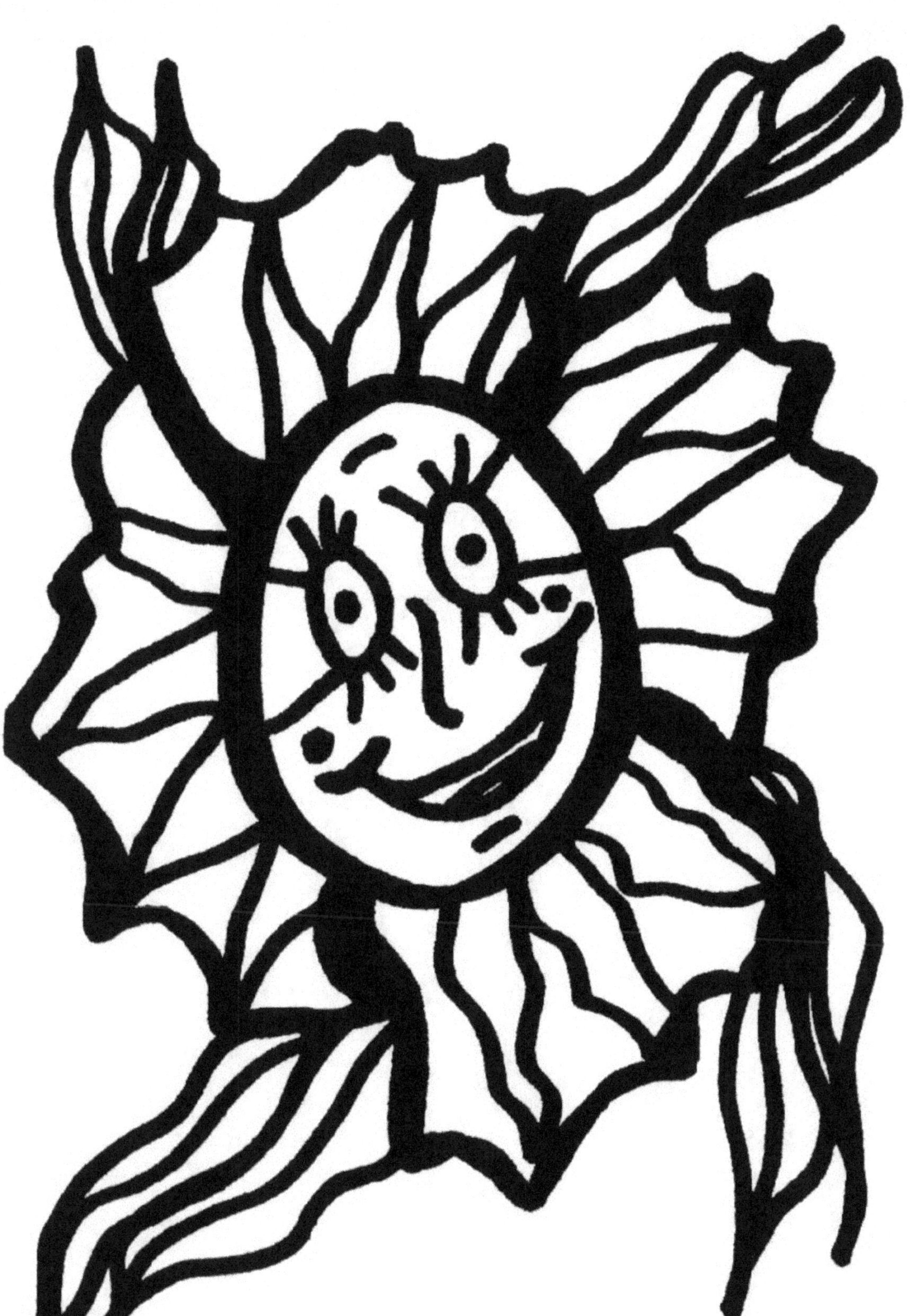

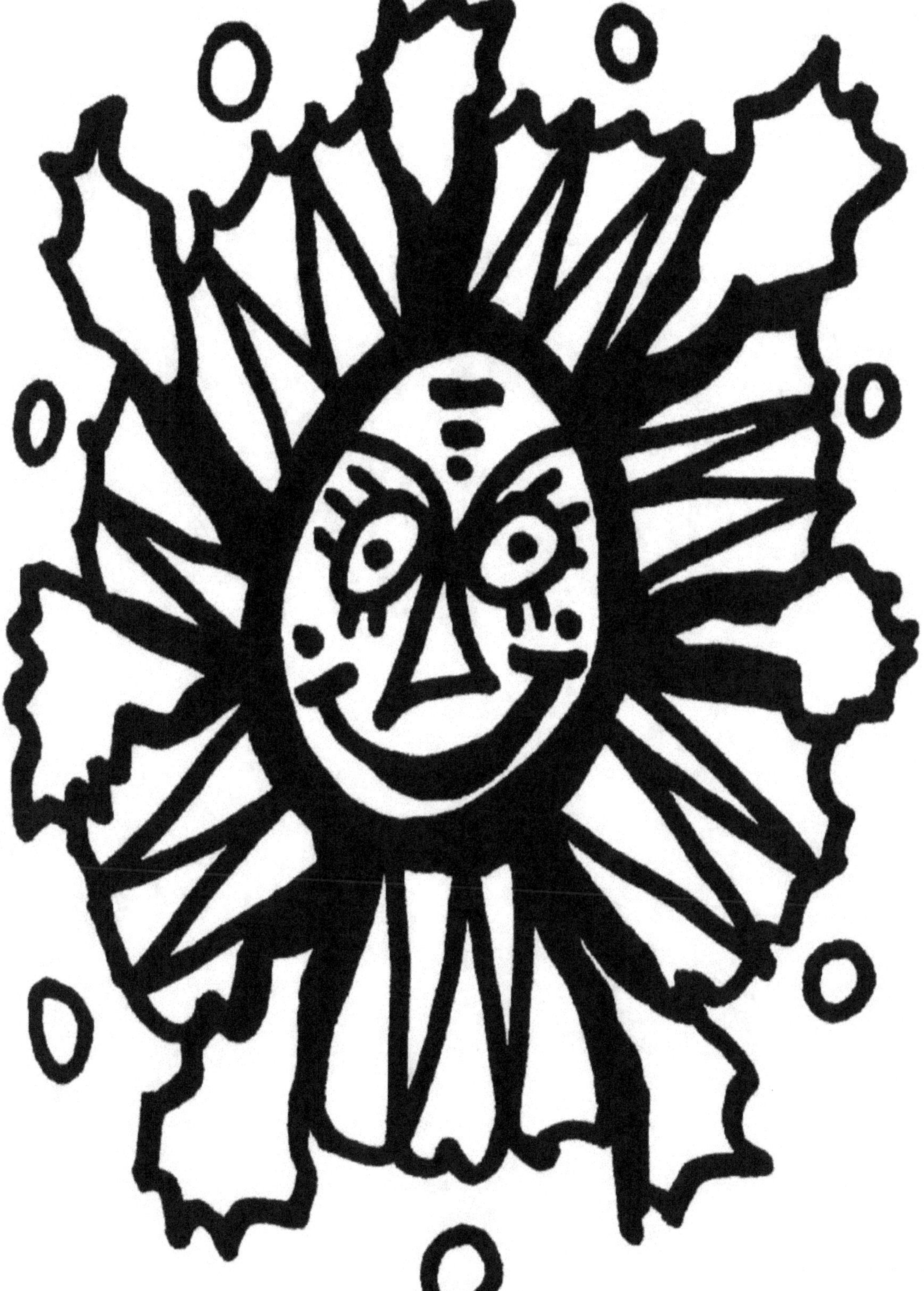

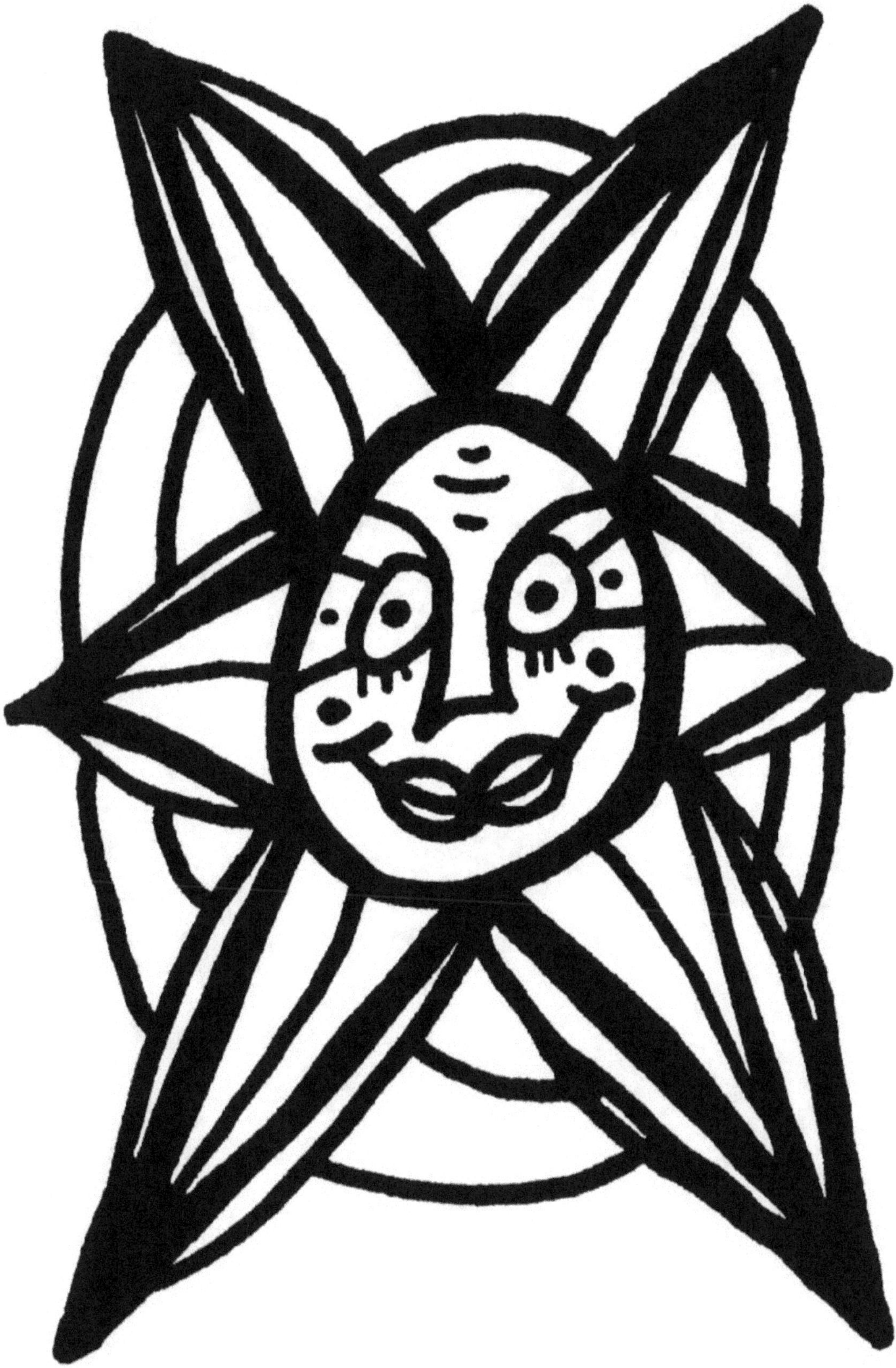

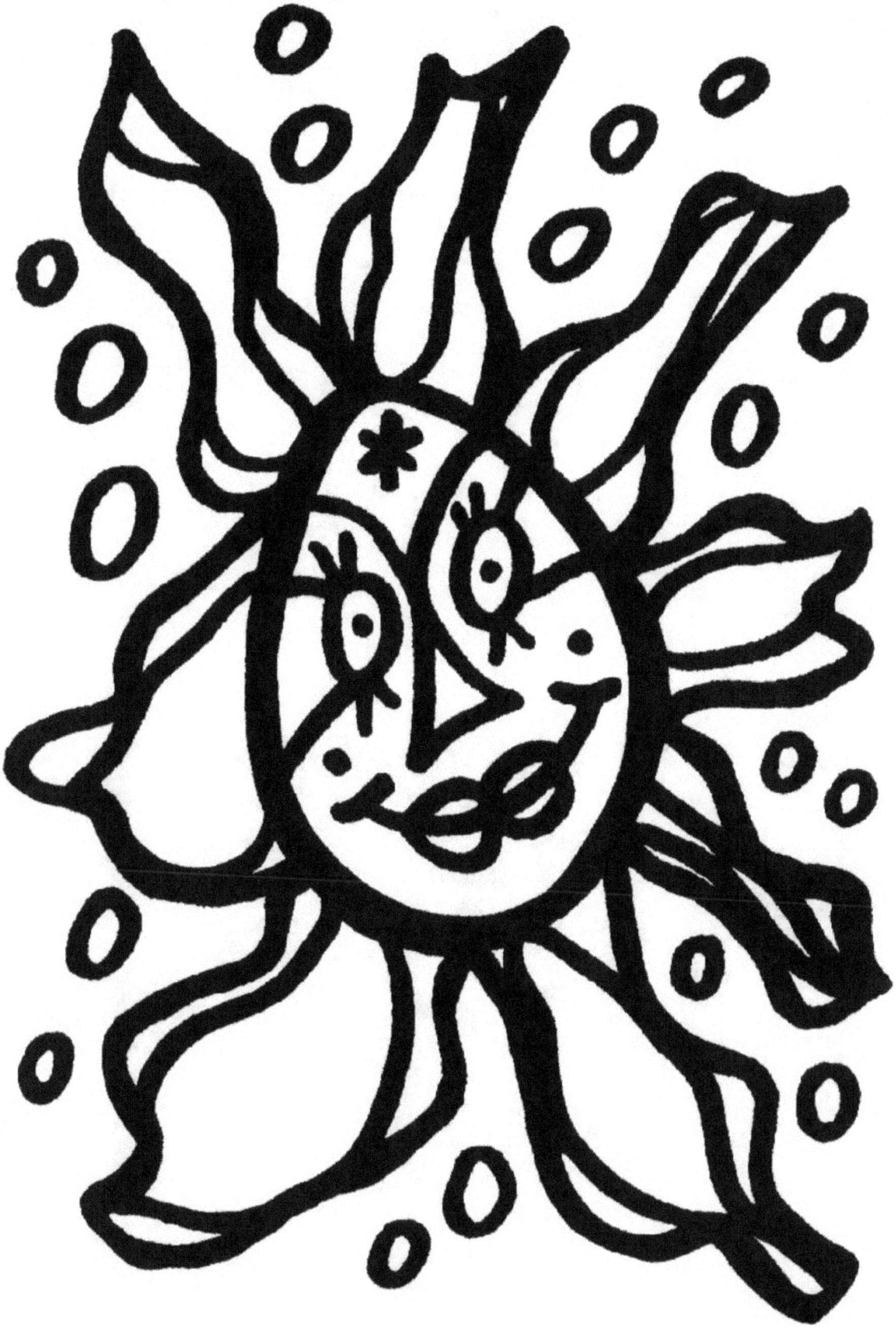

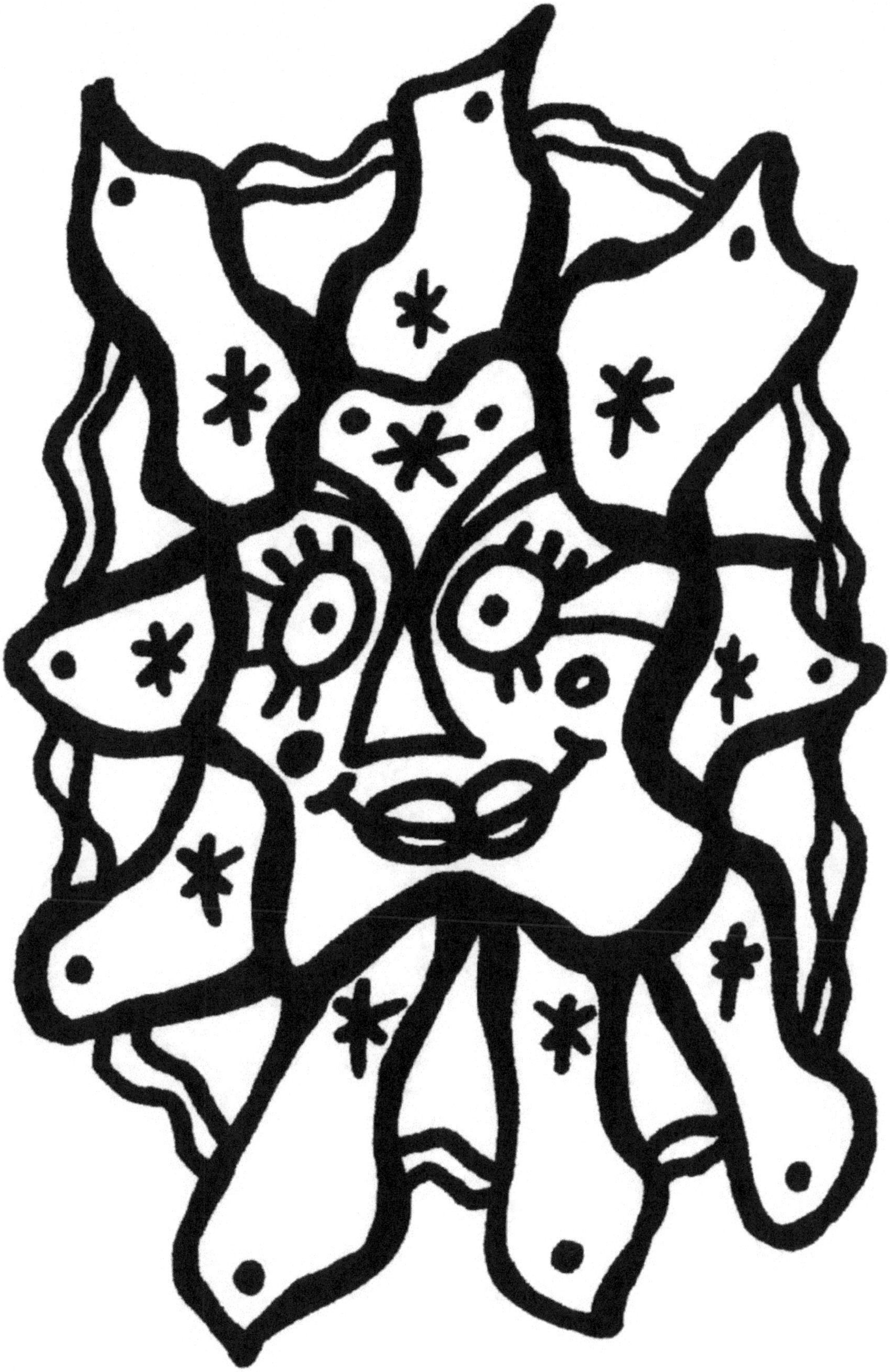

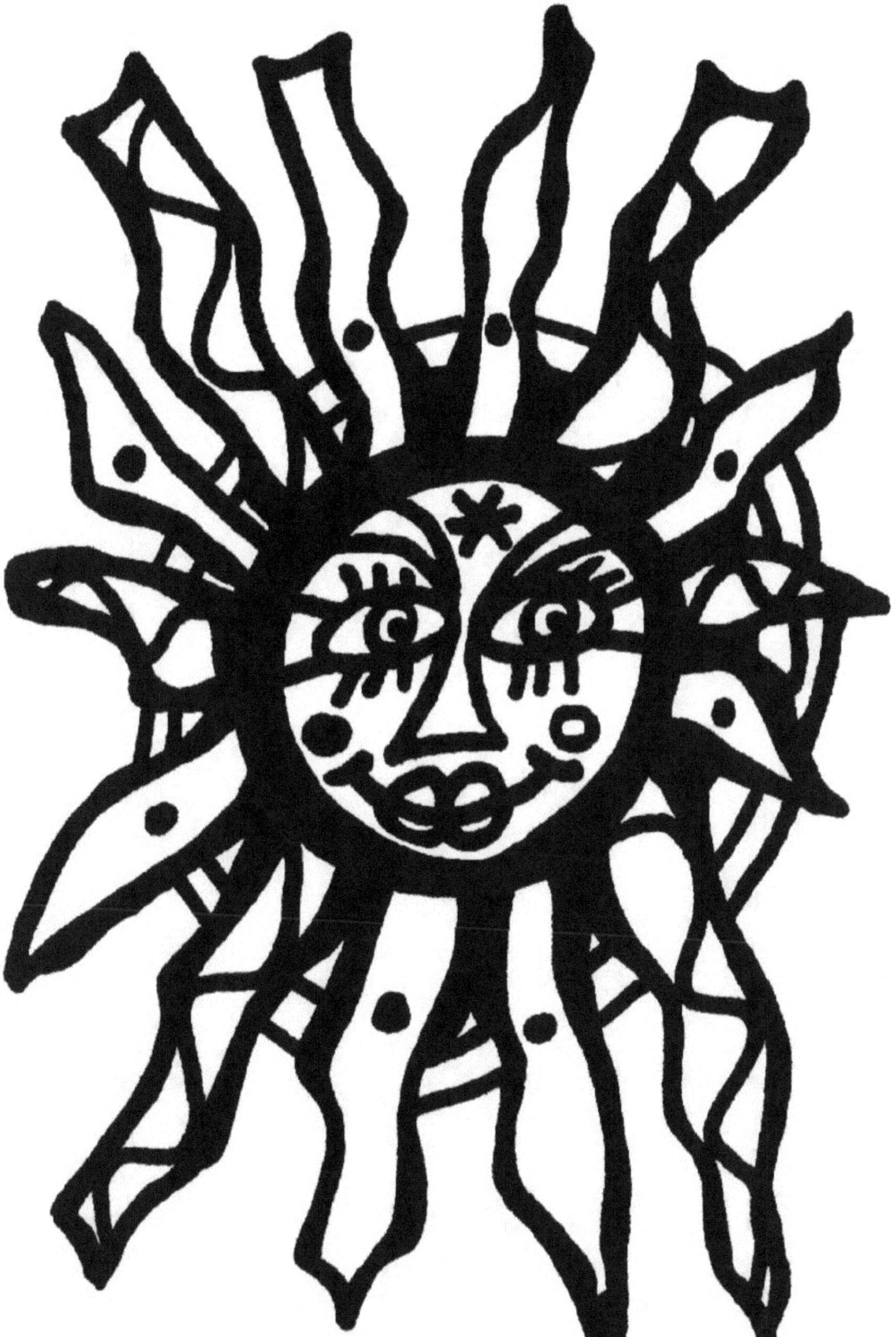

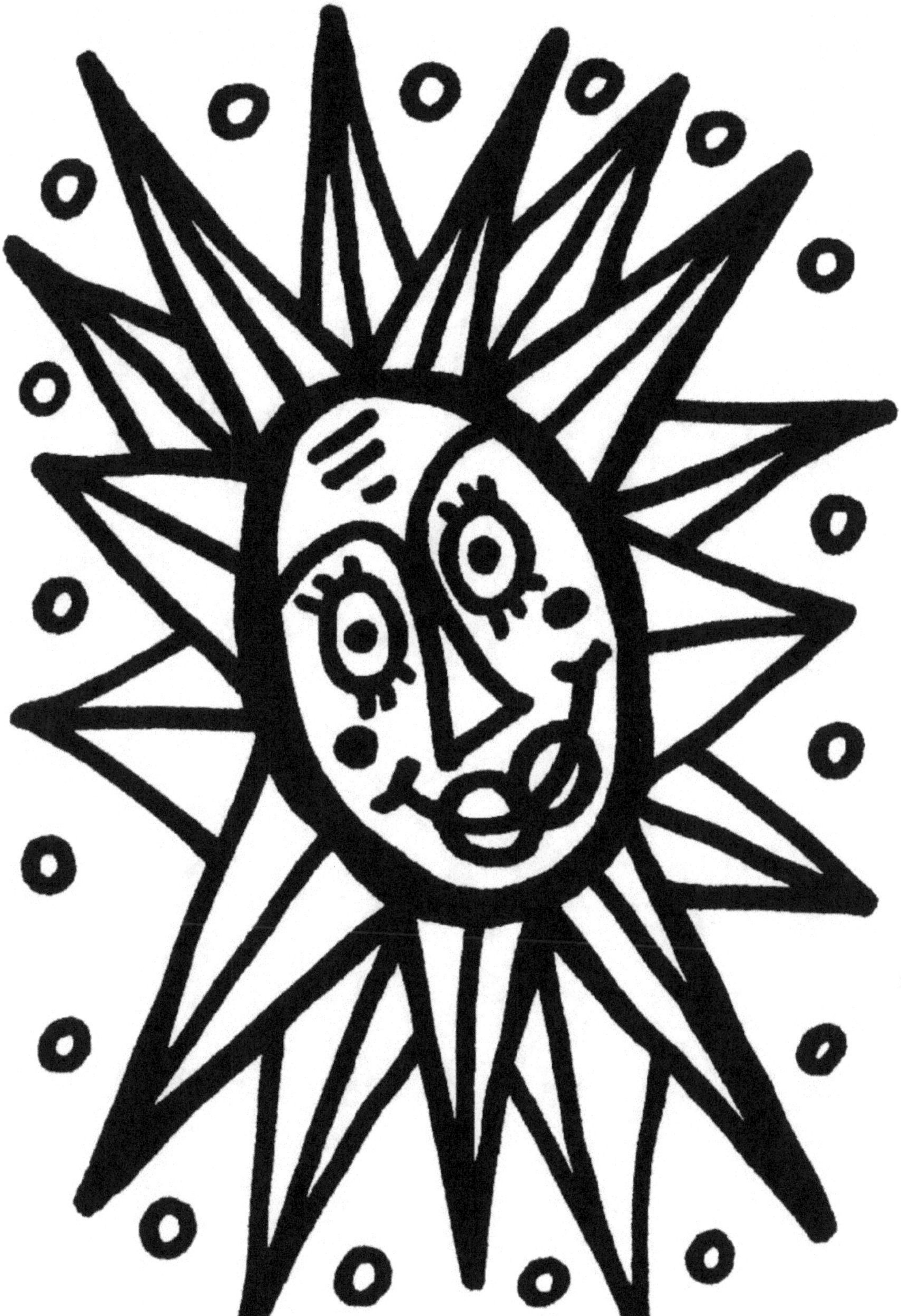

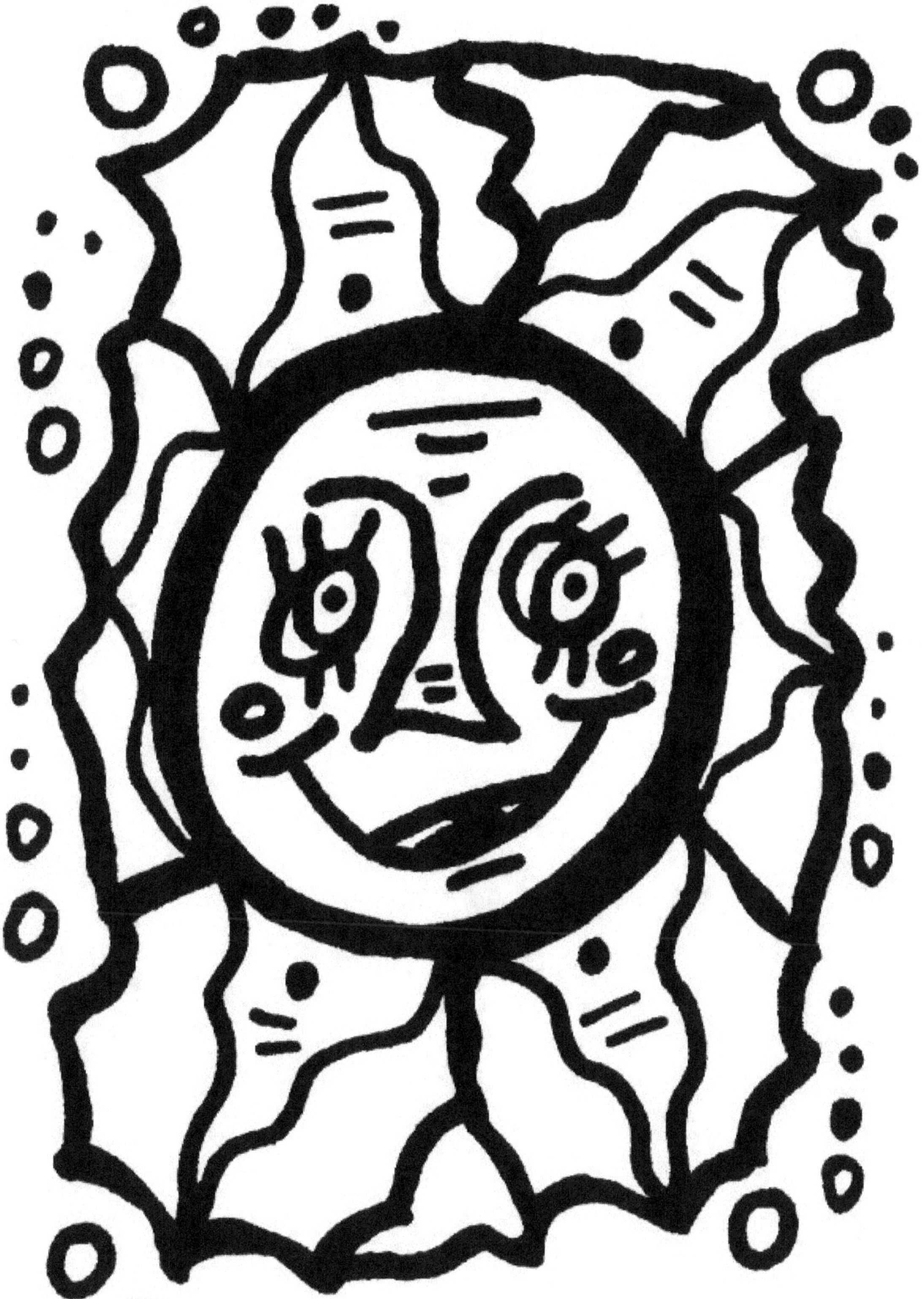

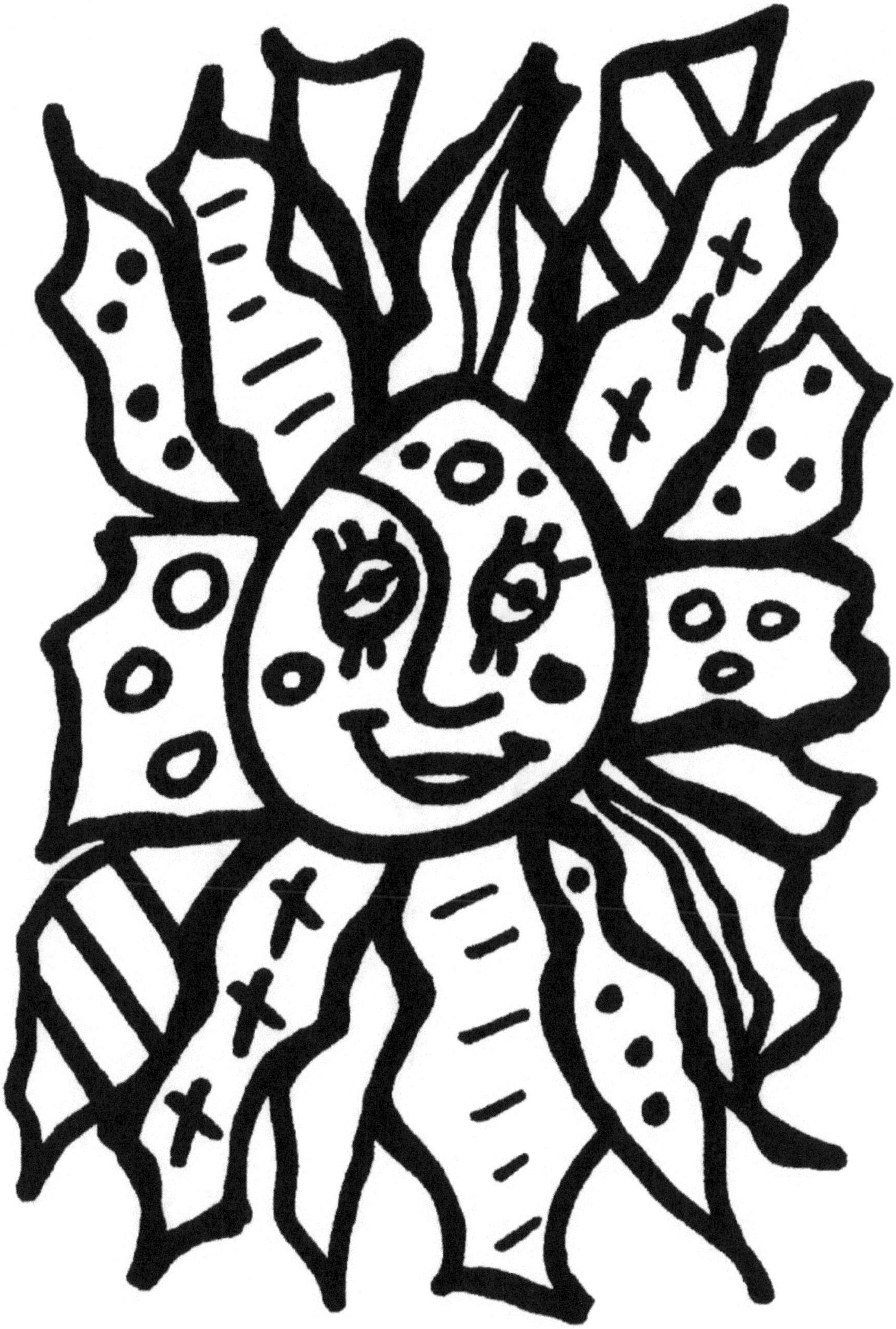

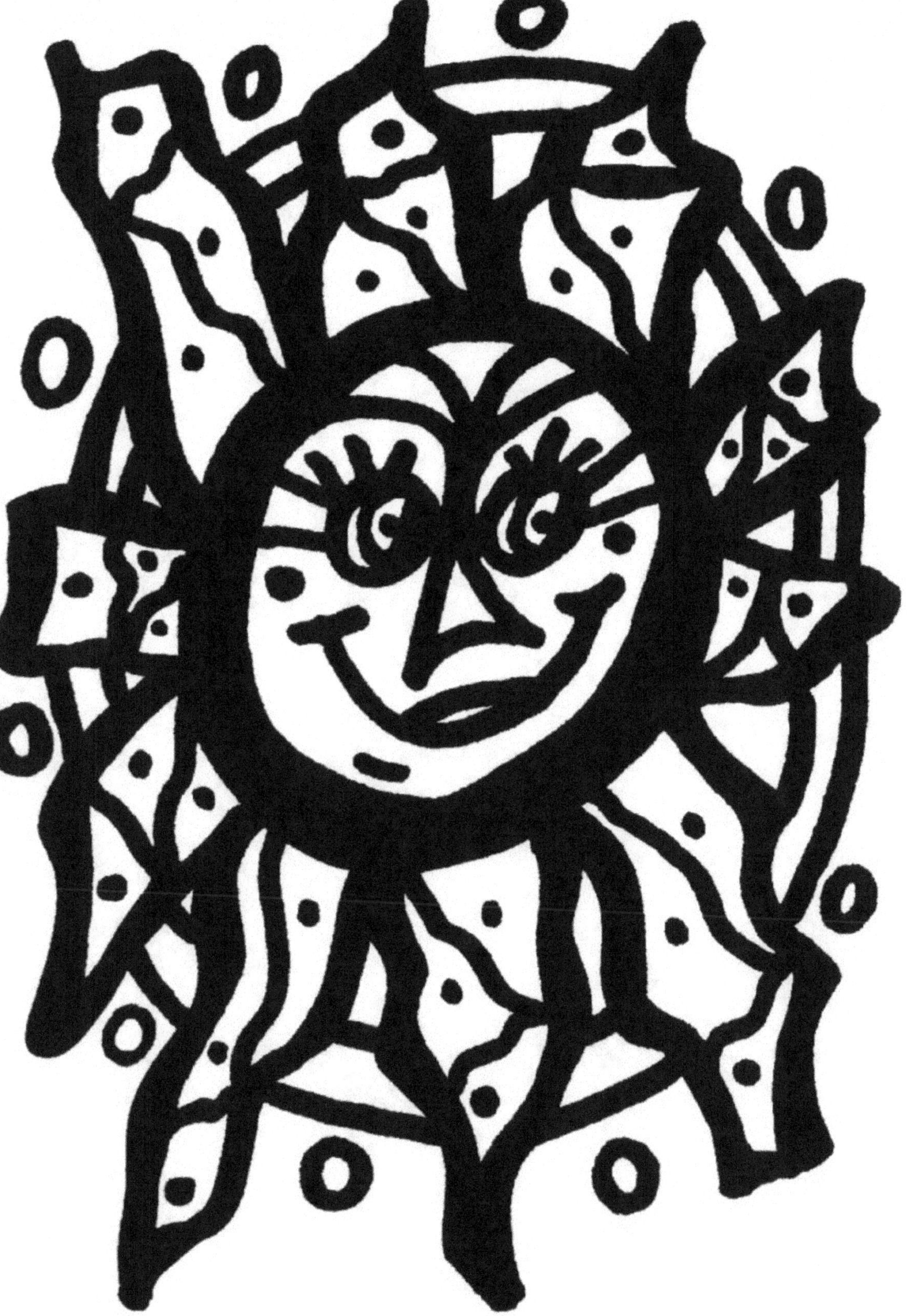

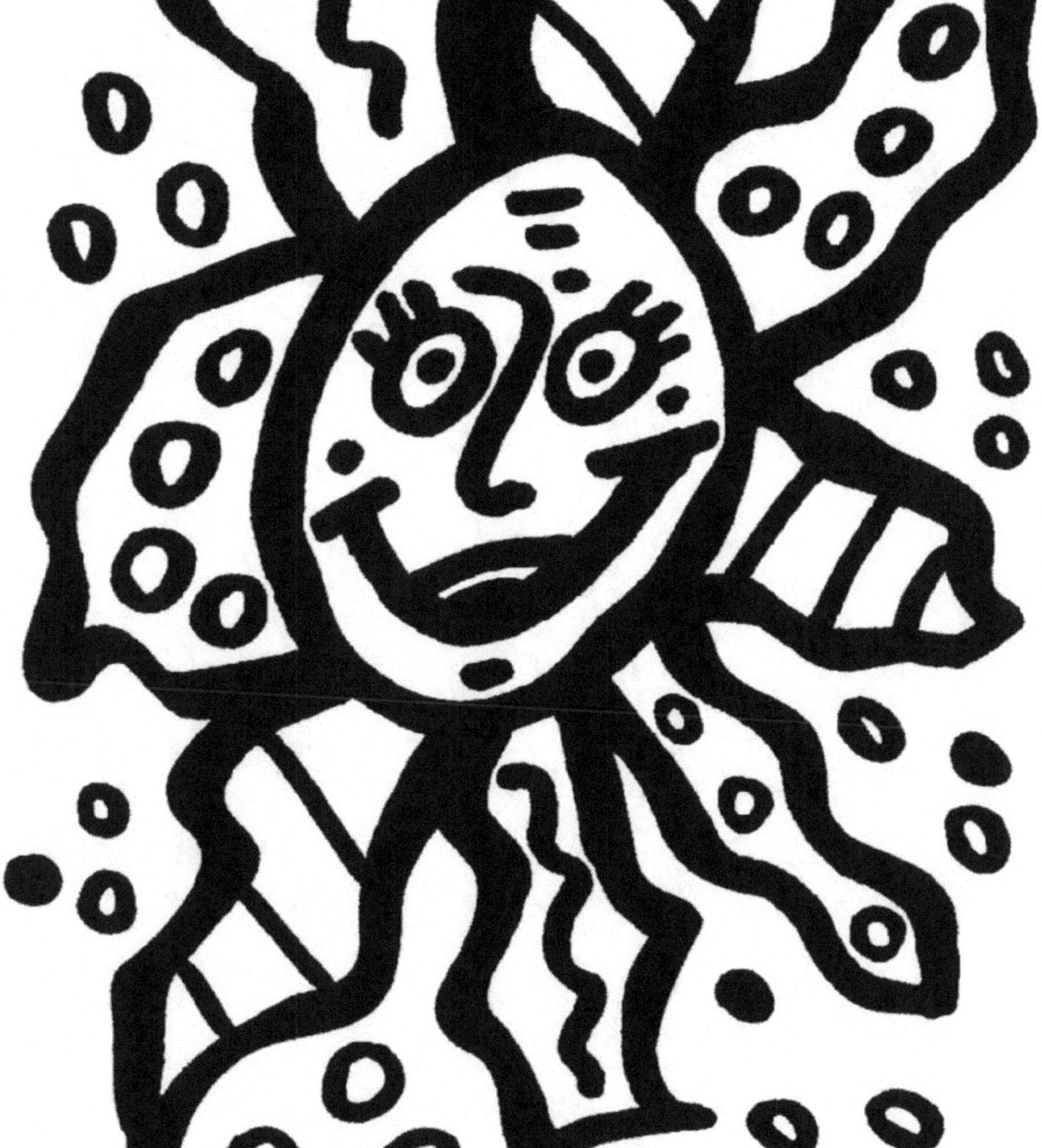

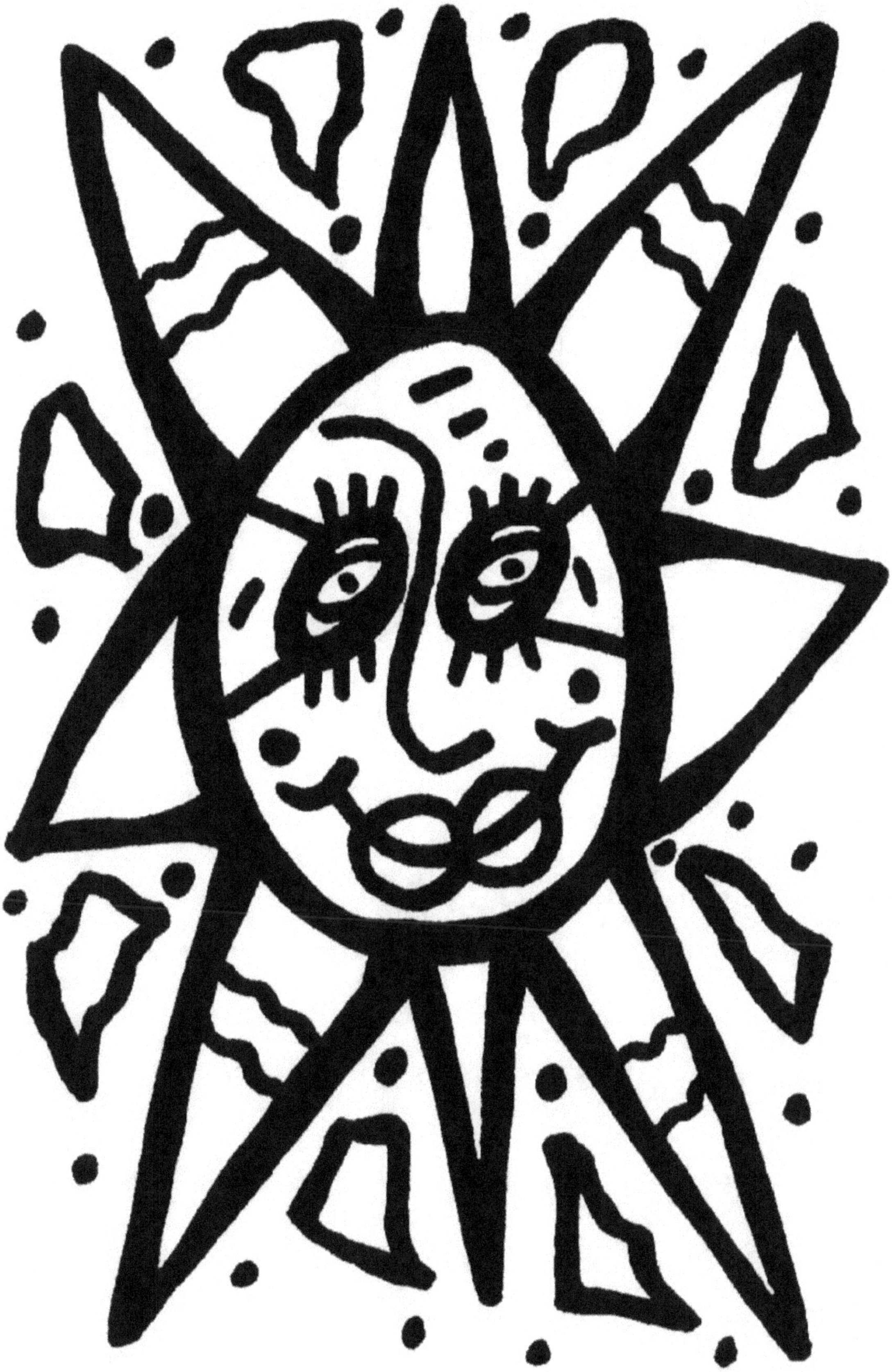

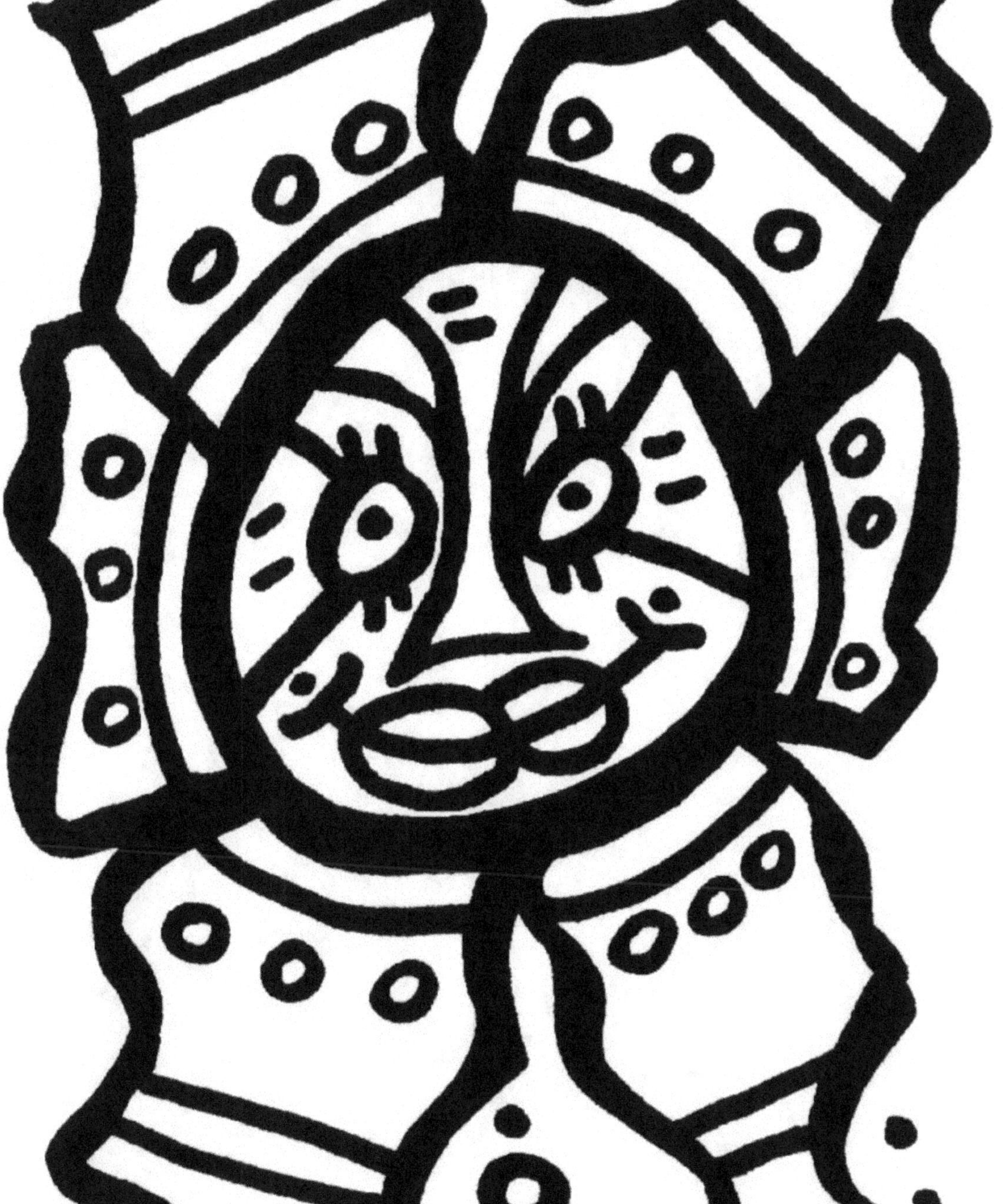

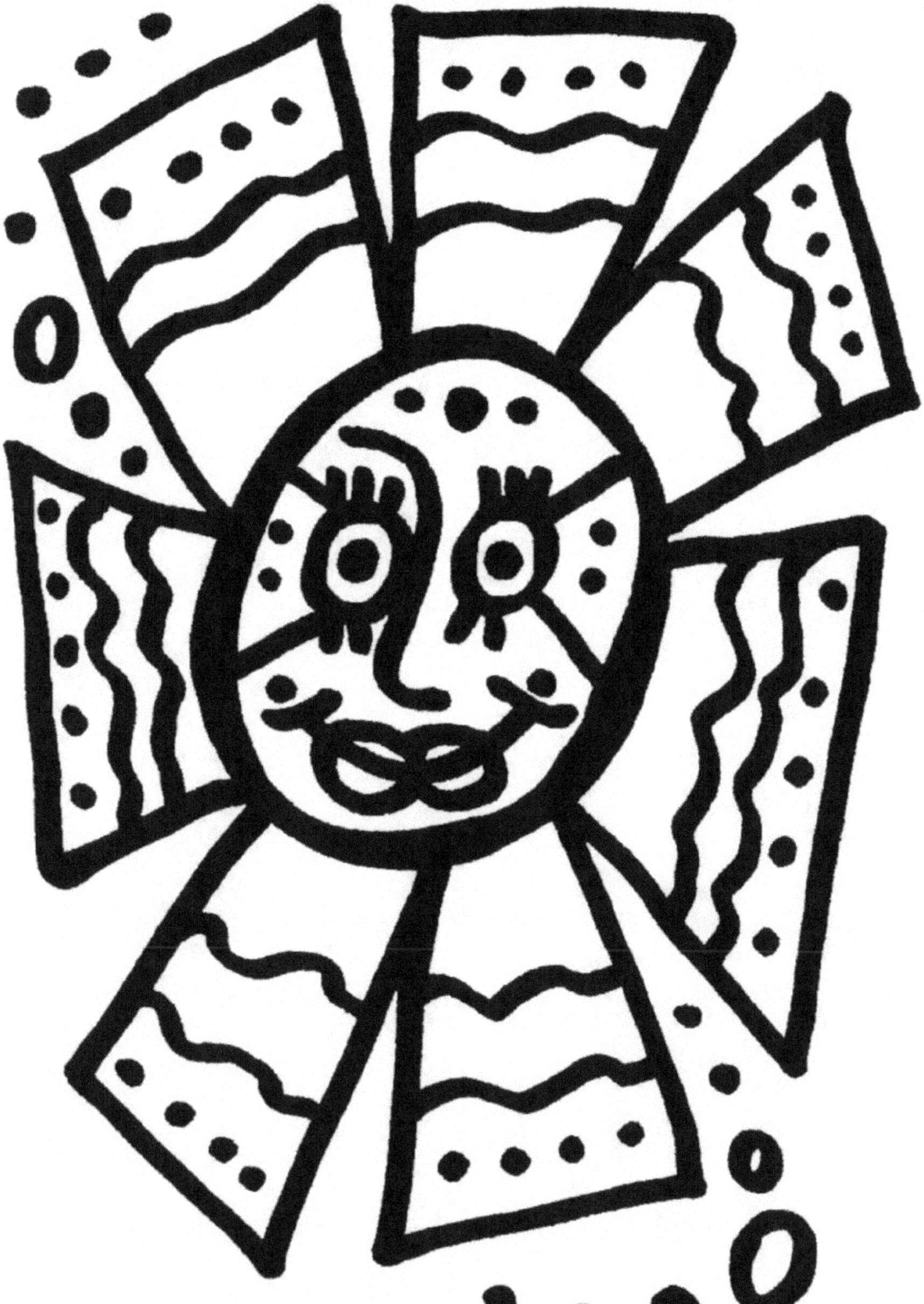

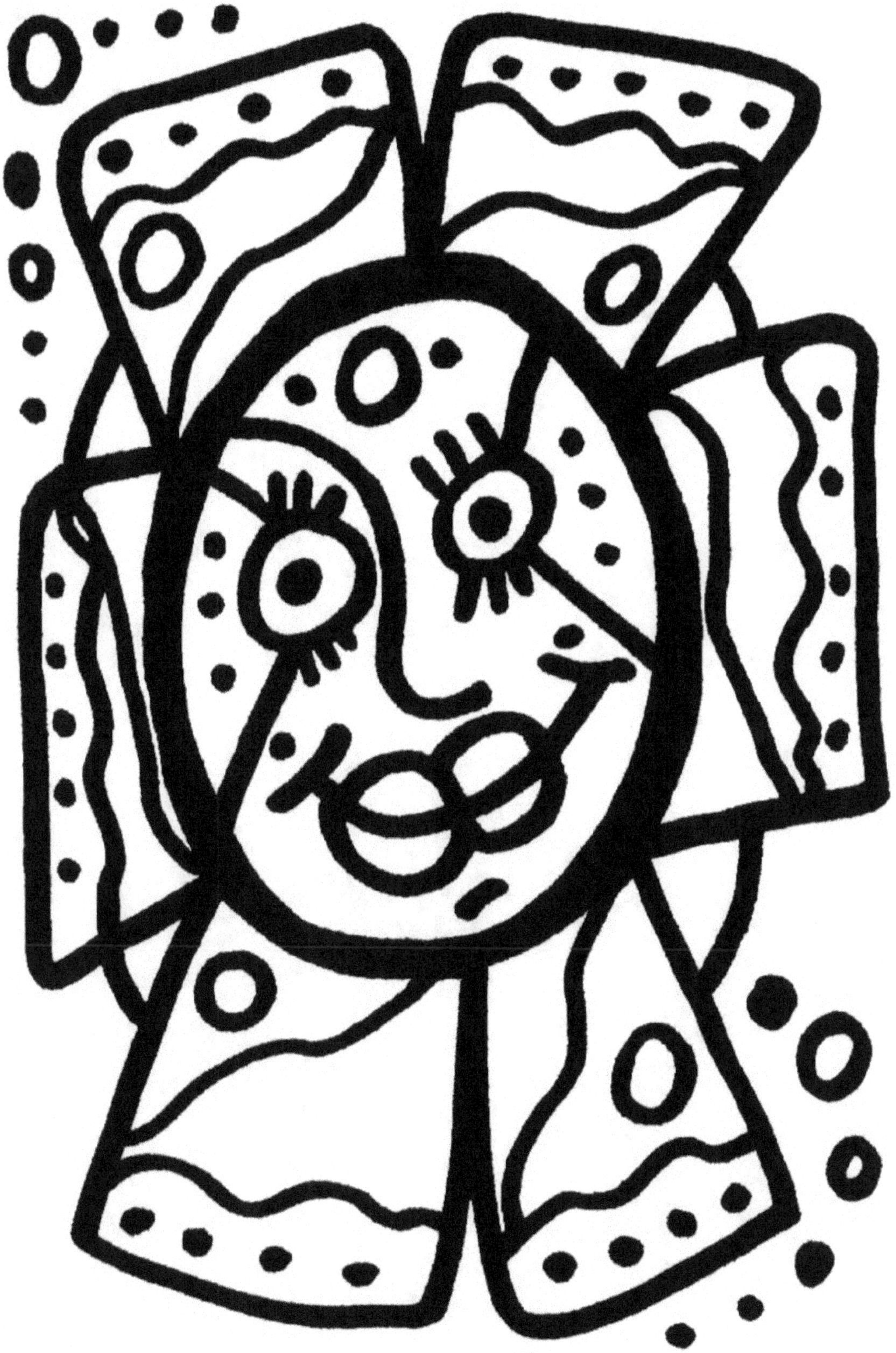

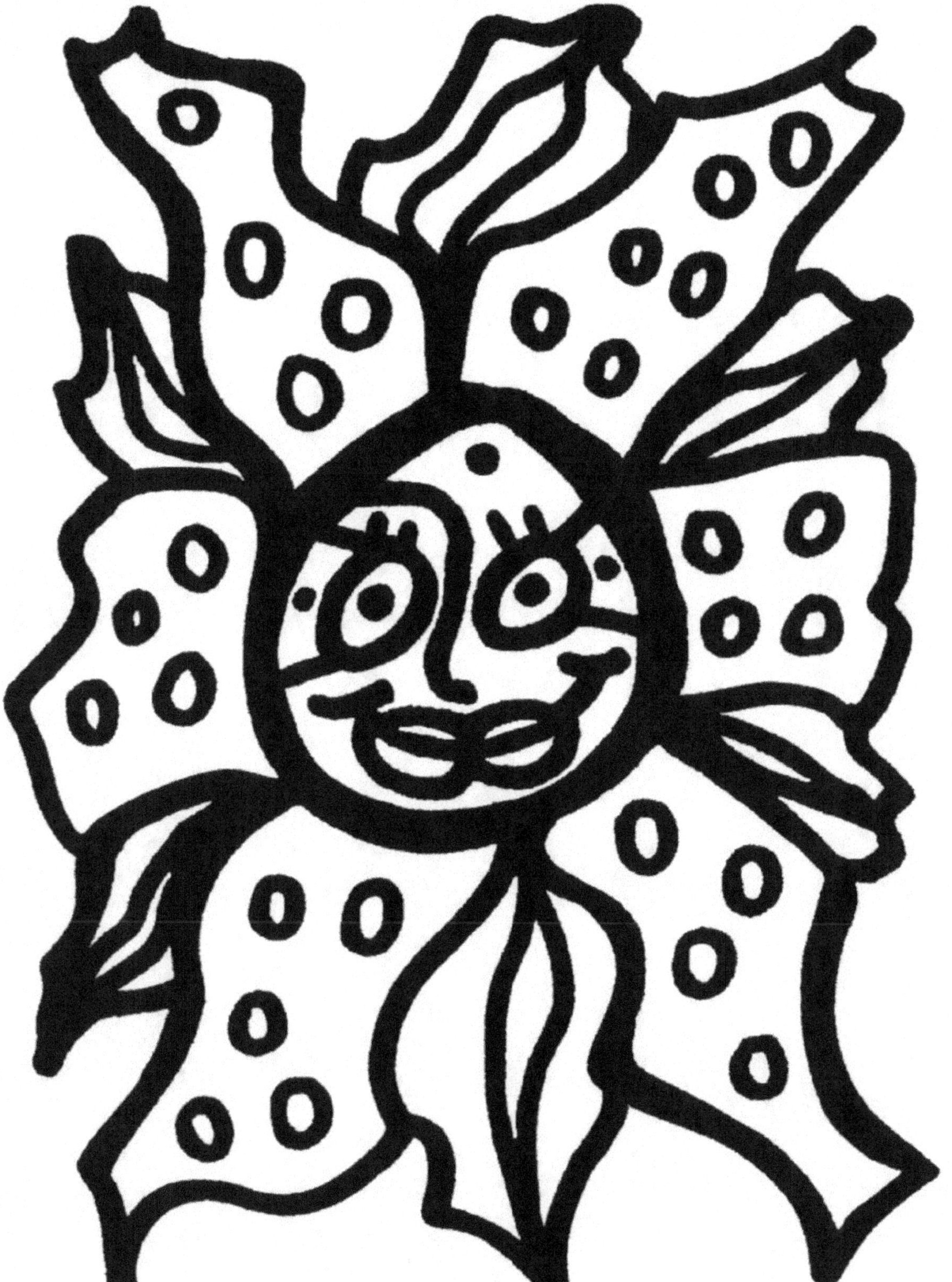

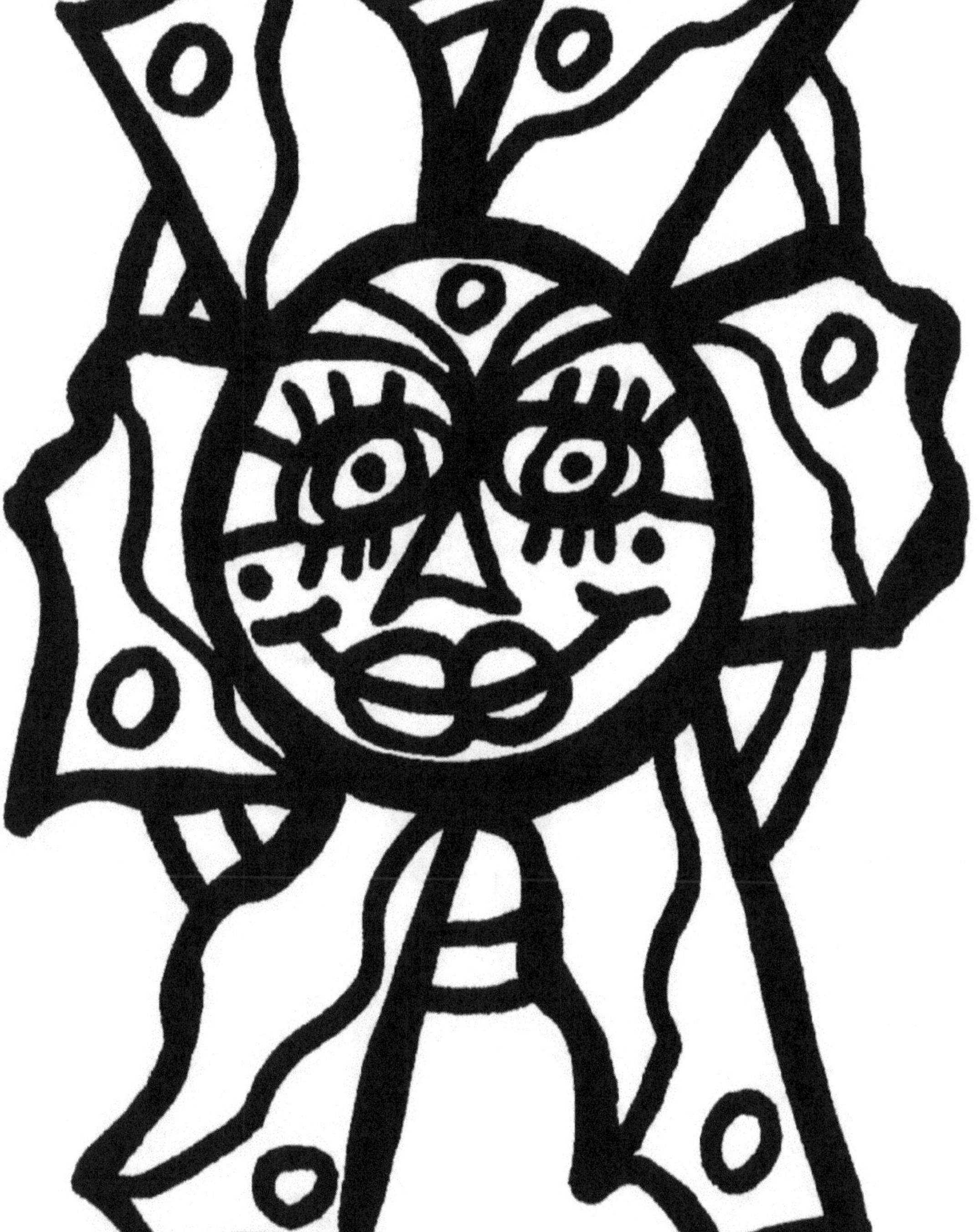

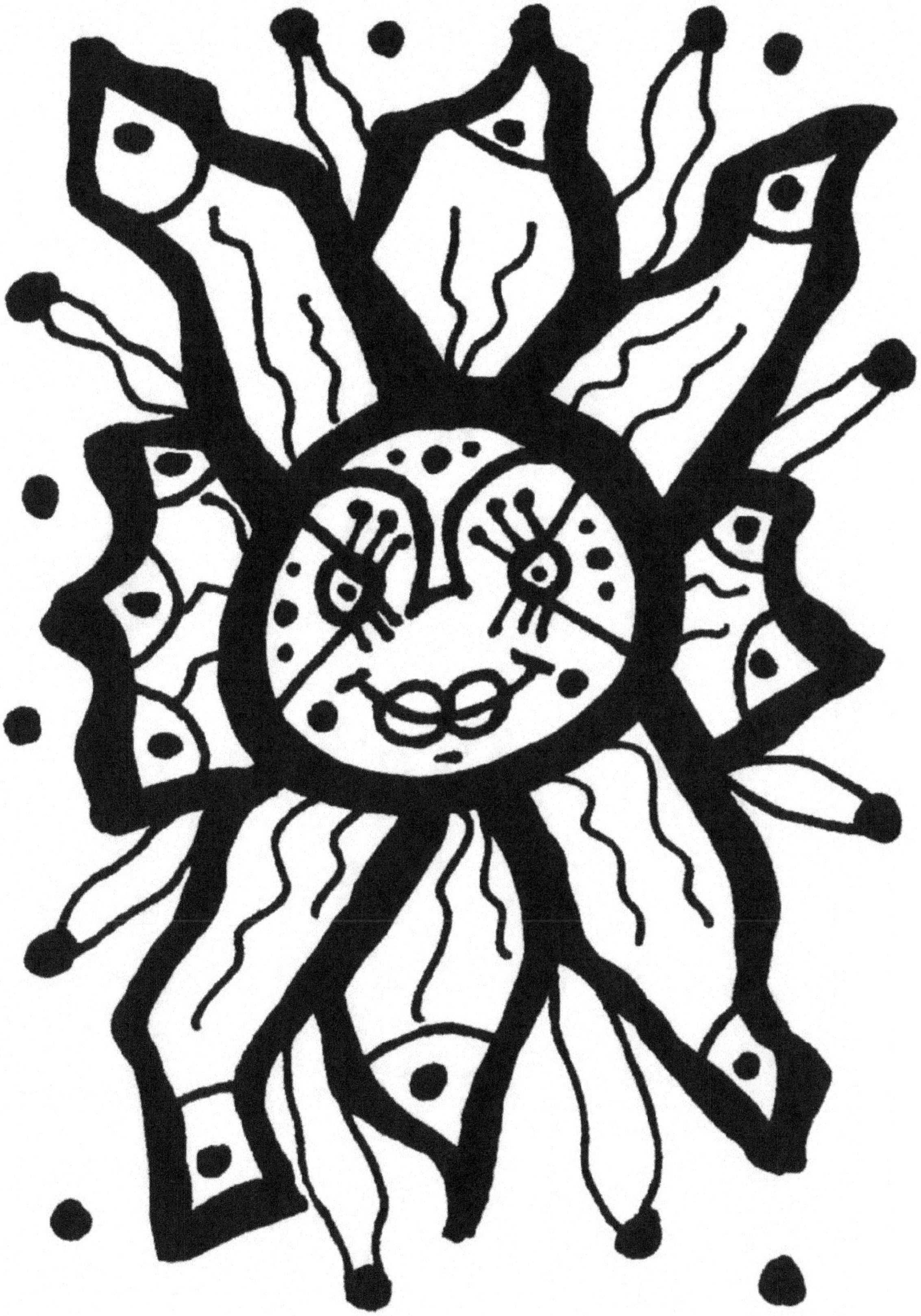

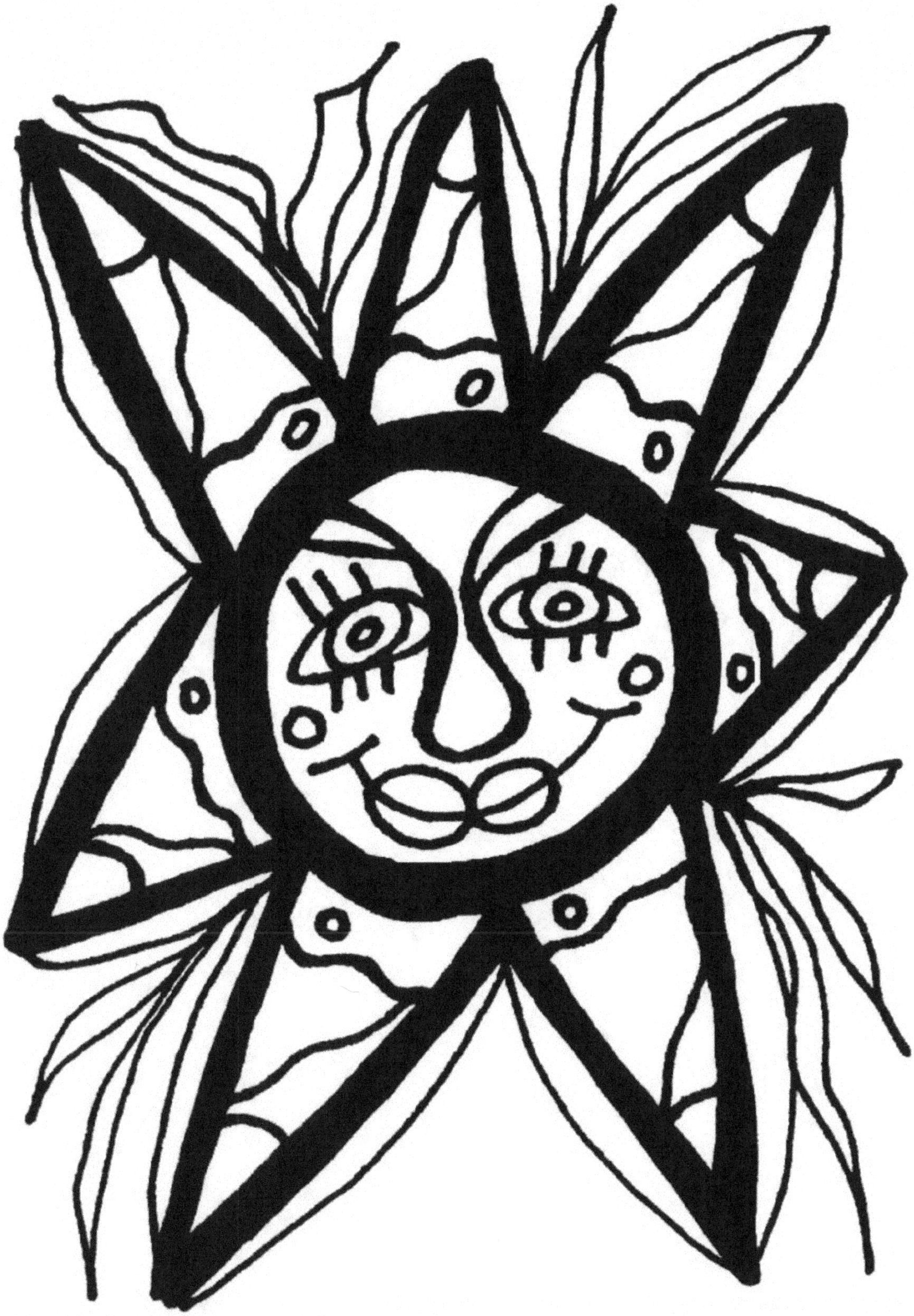

www.ingramcontent.com/pod-product-compliance
Lightning Source LLC
Chambersburg PA
CBHW081614170526
45166CB00009B/2956